IN THE HOLLOW OF HIS HAND

In the Hollow of His Hand

Devotions for Times of Adversity

BY KAI JENSEN

Translated by
Bernhard H. J. Habel

AUGSBURG PUBLISHING HOUSE
MINNEAPOLIS, MINNESOTA

Library of Congress Catalog Card No. 62-20844

This volume is a translation of the Danish Book, *Alt staar i Guds Faderhaand,* published in 1961 by J. Frimodts Forlag, Copenhagen, Denmark. Translations of some of the hymn stanzas are taken from *Hymnal for Church and Home,* Lutheran Publishing House, Blair, Neb., 1938. Others are original translations by Harriet Lucas Overholt.

MANUFACTURED IN THE UNITED STATES OF AMERICA

Foreword

Kai Jensen tells in the foreword to the Danish edition his purpose in writing these devotions. He says, "In this little book of 36 short chapters an attempt has been made to speak simply and clearly to persons too tired, too lonesome, or too infirm to care to read long-drawn-out discussions."

Indications are that many of us in the English speaking world are either bored, frustrated, or in despair. We get advice from many quarters on how to handle our problems and how to get release from tensions. We seek advice from the psychologist and are encouraged to talk them out. We go to the corner store to buy the latest advertised drug which is guaranteed to give a new lease on life. New techniques are offered by the medical doctor and there is renewed interest in pastoral psychology. We are apparently seeking solutions to our fears and anxieties.

In one of his essays, Kai Jensen writes, "The real problem is not how to get rid of anxiety, but how to let Christ have more power within us. No one on earth has the right to say with authority, 'You need not be afraid.' We are all afraid."

Bishop Jensen speaks to the questions in our minds and directs us to God who knows our distress. "Only one has both the right and the power to banish anxiety—Jesus Christ. The closer we live to him day by day, the greater strength we shall have to stand fast when the evil times come."

This book can help us in our devotional life that we may be strengthened when we are perplexed and given new hope when we are in despair.

William Larsen

Contents

1

Finding Rest

We are called to live a better life than is possible for us. We have aspirations which we cannot fulfill. Destructive forces beset us, and we are helpless. We want to be good, but we fail. We want to stand fast, but we slip and fall. We want to help and comfort, but we fall short. We want to live in the light, but we are lost in darkness. We want to live, but we have to die. This is the situation of all of us. How then is it possible for us to find rest?

First of all, we must understand that there is a difference between tranquility and rest. "Just take it easy now," said the rich farmer. He never got to the point of taking it easy himself, but that is another matter. It is not enough for anyone to take his ease. With the help of tranquilizers anyone can get to sleep, but what good does it do if one must wake up to greater pain?

There is only one way to find rest, and that is the way of Jesus Christ, who comes to us from the other side. We go, but he comes. We are from below; he is from above. We are bound, but his hands are free. "Come to me," he says, "and I will give you rest."

The most important word in Christianity is "Come!" It is heard directly or indirectly in all the preaching of Jesus. The parable of the Prodigal Son, the parable of the Great Supper, the parable of the Barren Fig Tree—what are they all but expressions of God's great invitation: "Come!" A call to us who have gone astray; an invitation to us who are lost; an out-stretched hand to helpless people called to live beyond their strength! "Come, and I will give you rest," says Jesus. When we do not know where to turn, when all the roads seem barred, when burdens bring us to our knees, when there seems no one to guide us through the darkness, when we are crushed by the thought of our guilt and responsibility—then we hear this "Come!" And he who calls us is the same yesterday, today, and forever.

In all truth, it must be said that there will always be some disquiet along with the peace that comes through faith. There are several reasons. For one thing, we have an enemy who will steal our rest if he can. Doesn't he pursue us with his devilish "What if—?" What if your faith is nothing but a delusion? What if God grows tired of you? What if your peace cannot last through times of adversity? These are ways by which he tries to undermine our faith.

There is some danger, too, in the very fact that our rest is bound up with our *faith.* Rest is not an inanimate possession that can be stored up. Our rest is found in Jesus, in his word, in his promises, in his faithfulness. Everything, then, depends upon our relation with him.

Besides all this, we are inclined to think that we cannot find peace without understanding the mysteries of life. If we could only get an answer whenever we ask, "Why?"—then we think we could find rest.

But it is not so. Relief does not come through explanations. Our peace is found in love as it is revealed in Jesus Christ. He is our Redeemer, and he can give us peace.

"Take my yoke upon you, and learn of me; for I am gentle and lowly in heart, and you will find rest for your souls," says Jesus (Matt. 11:29). By means of a yoke one can carry heavy burdens. One could, of course, call the yoke itself a burden; but it is a helpful burden.

What does Jesus mean by the yoke? Doesn't he mean the new way, the way of faith, the way of gentleness and meekness? The yoke is the way of God's will. That is a good way; that is the way we find rest; that is the way that leads us home.

The way of Jesus is lighted by hope; and whether the world will admit it or not, the truth is that life without hope is life without rest.

A little longer we must keep
Our course ere rest we earn;
Then death is just a little sleep,
As we from slumber learn.
The peace we taste so briefly here
We'll know midst songs of praises clear,
Beyond earth's cares and sadness,
In heaven's eternal gladness.

GRUNDTVIG

2

On Solid Ground

"Can you help me? I have two big boys at home, and I wish I could reach far enough to tell them that I have had a firm foundation for my life. How can I do it?" So spoke a patient in a hospital, knowing that he did not have much longer to live.

Where does one find a safe foundation?

Not in ourselves! No matter how hard we try, our own efforts will never be enough. Some people may take exception to this statement, but it is true. The Pharisees were angry when Jesus said that it was the sick—not the well—who needed a physician. Were they perhaps sick? No, they depended on themselves, on their righteousness. They had no need of a physician.

Where do we find the firm foundation? Paul says, "For no other foundation can anyone lay than that which is laid, which is Jesus Christ" (1 Cor. 3:11).

What does this mean? It means that God himself clears the ground and lays a new foundation. Indeed, he did so by sending his own Son. Thus he changed the whole situation and set us in a new environment. The means of our salvation has been given us in Jesus Christ. He engaged in battle with our enemy and won. He has paid what had to be paid; nothing extra has to be added. It has all been done.

Our sure foundation is God's word of grace. "And now I commend you to God and to the word of grace, which is able to build you up, and to give you an inheritance among all those who are sanctified" (Acts 20:32). These were Paul's words when he bade farewell to the elders of the congregations in Asia Minor. "In all dangers we rely on God's grace and build securely," says Grundtvig.

We must believe in the magnitude of God's grace and take care not to belittle it. Grace means love unearned or unmerited. It is undeserved compassion. How great it is! "To the thirsty I will give water without price from the fountain of the water of life" (Rev. 21:6). "Since all have sinned and fall short of the glory of God, they are justified by his grace as a gift, through the redemption which is in Christ Jesus" (Rom. 3:23, 24). *As a gift*—that is the word that saves us.

You may ask if there are not certain conditions, if one should not repent and believe, if one should not have certain experiences. The answer is—what could a prodigal son have to offer? Wasn't the father's love there before the boy returned home? No, in speaking of God's grace, we cannot use the word "condition." Yet it does not operate automatically; God's grace is sometimes offered in vain.

When the sun is shining from blue skies, if I am sitting in my office with the shades down, I must raise the shades before I can take my place in the sun. Raising the shades does not make the sun shine, but I must raise them to have the sun's rays reach me. I can shut myself out from the sunshine, but I cannot keep the sun from shining.

Pull up the shades! Let the sun shine in!

Yes, but how do I know that God's grace applies to me?

God told you so the moment that you were baptized. In the grace of infant baptism the firm and sure foundation is laid. At the beginning of your life God gives you the word of his grace, and he does not go back on his word. You may have it confirmed at the Lord's table. In the Holy Supper, God's free grace is given anew to each individual.

It is good to be able to say, "He . . . set my feet upon a rock, making my steps secure. He put a new song in my mouth, a song of praise to our God" (Ps. 40:2b, 3a).

The ground on which I'm building
Is Jesus and his death,
His cross's shadow yielding
Sweet peace as I draw breath;
There new life I am finding,
Though I am nothing worth,
Christ's gift God's love is binding
To me in my rebirth.

BRORSON

3

Not One Is Forgotten by God

Many years ago I visited a mother who was dying. She lingered a long time and suffered much pain; but this period of waiting became one of blessed significance for her. She had not given much thought to God. She was a good woman who had spent her time caring for her husband and her children. But now it was different. She got a Bible and began to read it. She began to talk to God in prayer; and we had many talks together about the way that leads to eternal life.

On the day of her death I called on her husband. He was reading his wife's new Bible when I came in.

"Is what I read in this book true?" he asked.

"Why do you ask me that today?"

"I happened to open the book, and I came upon a sentence I cannot get away from."

It proved to be some words from the twelfth chapter of Luke where Jesus says, "And not one of them is forgotten before God" (Luke 12:6b).

"Is this true?" the man asked.

"Yes, it is true."

No one is forgotten by God. It is hard for us to

realize that. What can one little human being mean among the multitudes of God's creatures? Do I dare believe that God loves even me? "I am lonely and insignificant," you may say; "I am almost a burden. Who would ever bother about me? No, that's too much for me to believe."

Nonetheless it is true. Jesus told the story of the man who had a hundred sheep and lost one of them. What did he do? Did he say, "What does it matter—one sheep more or less?" No, he went out, risking himself to find the sheep that was lost; and when he had found it, he laid it across his shoulders and carried it home. Why did Jesus tell this story? So that we could understand that not a single person is forgotten by God.

No one has the right to disregard this truth. We have no right to be ungrateful to the Creator who gave us life and who allowed Jesus to die so that not one of us need perish.

After all, how can we tell? A person who thinks himself of no account may have had great influence on the lives of others. Some whose names never appeared in the papers until their obituaries were printed may have had their names inscribed in the hearts of men and women they had helped by prayer and example to find the right way of life.

"I know where you dwell." Thus speaks the Lord to one church in the last book of the Bible" (Rev. 2:13). And God knows where you dwell. That goes not only for churches but for every human being.

You are not out of his sight or his reach, and he will never forget you. He wants to bring you home.

In the world, it is true, one individual means very little. Our names are forgotten like the snow that fell last year. But God is God. His reckonings are different from ours. To him every individual has inestimable worth. So it is wrong—it is even heresy—for anyone to say that he himself does not count.

Thank God, all of you, for his gift of life. Give thanks that you can believe that no one is forgotten by God. Then perhaps you will find the sun breaking through the clouds and you will feel like singing a hymn in God's praise.

Your Father in heaven
To you has given
A brother and Savior in Jesus, his Son.
Trustfully stand
Clasping his hand;
He'll lead you onward, your victory won!

ROSENIUS

4

To Whom Shall We Go?

The Bible speaks plainly. It describes human beings who struggle and fall. It reveals the darkness and the evil in the world. Realistically, it teaches that when man is left to himself, he is subject to sin and death.

But the Bible is also man's most consoling book. It helps us face our battles courageously. In spite of the power of evil, we can resist with confidence. Why? Because Christ once walked this earth and because he still lives. "Be of good cheer," he says, "I have overcome the world" (John 16:33b).

We can easily understand the impulsive confession of Simon Peter: "Lord, to whom shall we go? You have the words of eternal life" (John 6:68). If we could ask Peter what he meant by these words, he might not be able to give a clear answer, but he knew that in Jesus he had found something different from anything else he had ever known.

Simon Peter was, like us, a man of flesh and blood. He meant well, but he did not always think before he spoke. He had left his fishing boat to follow Jesus. Who Jesus was he was not sure of then, but he wanted to be near him. When others fell away because they were offended at Jesus' calling himself the Bread of Life, Peter felt compelled to make this confession of his own faith, beginning with a question, "Lord, to whom shall we go?"

Well, to whom shall *we* go? We have no place here on earth to go in the hour of need. The strongest and wisest cannot save us. They may leave us all alone with our perplexities. Our families, of course, might want to say or do something to help, but they too are powerless. To whom can we turn?

When sin accuses us and we have no defense, to whom shall we go? Who can assure us with authority that we shall be forgiven? Jesus Christ can. He has authority to forgive sins on earth. On the cross at Golgotha he said, "It is finished."

We can refer our accusers to Jesus.

When fears overwhelm us, to whom can we go? Who can say to us, "Don't be afraid"? Everyone is afraid. Some who talk loud and appear to be heroes are really full of fears. They grow silent when they are asked to help us who are afraid. But Jesus can say, "Do not be afraid!" His are not empty words. "Let not your hearts be troubled," he said to his disciples on the last evening he was with them; "you believe in God, believe also in me" (John 14:1).

When lonesomeness and weariness distress us, to whom shall we go? We can visit with our friends for a while, but afterwards the loneliness is even more overwhelming. Above the bed of one elderly woman was a framed sampler with this message embroidered in capital letters, "Jesus went in to tarry with them." She was lonely and weak, but also happy and grateful. She knew to whom she was going. The risen Savior, who on the first Easter had come to the home of the disciples at Emmaus, was her refuge too, and she was not deserted. She was lonely, but not alone.

When thoughts of approaching death dismay us, to whom can we go? Not one of us fully understands death, but we know that its hour comes to each of us. How shall we make our way through the darkness? Christ has the words of eternal life. It is he who says, "I am the resurrection and the life; he who believes in me, though he die, yet shall he live" (John 11:25).

There's no one in this world at all
That can my sorrow heal
Excepting Thee, who at my call
Bring comfort that is real.
O Jesus dear, my need now see,
Who tasted bitter death for me
My blessedness to seal.

STHEN

5

The Riddles of Life

Mankind forever asks "Why?" or "What for?"
As we move on from problem to problem;
God's ways, above our ways; his wisdom, much more!
But the riddles—oh, we want to solve them.

JACOB PAULLI

Why are there so many unsolved problems in life? Why is it so hard to be a human being? Why doesn't God intervene with us since he is our omnipotent Father?

If one starts wondering about the riddles of life, he soon finds himself stuck. Of course there are some who think they can answer any question. But usually their answers are light or cheap and therefore worthless. It is better to admit that some riddles are unsolvable. God has not given us a list of answers, and Christianity does not promise to explain away all life's problems. We live by faith, not by explanations.

Besides, life on earth is fragmentary. We cannot arrange the pieces of its mosaic to form the whole design. Or, to use another figure, we see life's pattern from the wrong side where the knots and ends show, ruining the impression of the whole design. But that's what happens when we see things from the wrong side.

There are many questions for which we do not

need to find an answer. We are like impatient, curious children demanding clear-cut answers. But God has a different way of looking at it. "I cannot explain it all to you now," he says, "but a time may come when I can show you why it had to happen the way it did."

Yes, many questions may be left unanswered, but one thing we must understand. If we do not grasp it, we cannot breathe freely. We must know that *love* is the strongest force in our existence.

If darkness and evil become the conquering forces, we are lost.

If love is not fundamental in life, we must despair.

Here God has given us a direct answer. He so loved the world that he gave his only begotten Son; and even though the powers of darkness persuaded men to sentence love to death, they could not conquer love. After Good Friday came Easter morning. We *know* that love is the strongest force in the world.

As we ponder the riddles of life, we must find the right starting point. The enemy does everything in his power to overwhelm us. But we must repel him. God has given us a place to stand; when we find it, rifts will appear in the clouds. He who allowed Jesus to suffer and die, wants only the best for us. We can trust him. Yes, that is the one thing we can do.

Our Savior himself has known darkness. He asked, Why? Why? This "why" comes from the deepest darkness. It shows that no matter how black the darkness is that surrounds us, Jesus has known an even deeper darkness. And that means that there are footprints for us to follow. Jesus has walked there before us. He suffered; therefore he can stand by us when the enemy taunts us in the darkness of pain. "Follow me," says Jesus.

Oh, take my hand, dear Father,
And lead Thou me,
Till at my journey's ending
I dwell with Thee.
Alone I dare not journey
One single day,
So do Thou guide my footsteps
On life's rough way.

JULIA VON HAUSMANN

6

God Takes Care of All

"Are not two sparrows sold for a penny? And not one of them will fall to the ground without your Father's will. . . . Fear not, therefore; you are of more value than many sparrows" (Matt. 10:29, 31). These are words of Jesus, and we do well to listen to them.

They tell us that God is with us all the way. God is not the cause of everything that happens. We should not hasten to say, "Well, it is the will of God," when anything bewildering or tragic happens to us. We may think that we are expressing pious resignation with such words, but that is not right. God is not the cause of everything that happens in this mad world where the enemy of the soul drives with a loose rein. Much of what happens is against the will of God.

But Jesus said that not one sparrow falls to the ground without the Father's will. God is with us even in situations for which we or our fellow men are to blame. He lets them happen. Why, we cannot explain.

But God never abandons us. He lets the laws of nature work, for he himself ordered them. What a man sows he also reaps. That is one of God's laws. Still he knows everything that happens. When we are grieved because we see that we were at fault,

God shows that it can all be used in his plan for our salvation. If we submit ourselves to his will, he will use our mistakes for our final good.

What was it that Joseph said to his brothers? "You meant evil against me, but God meant it for good" (Gen. 50:20). Things can work out that way, for God's will is concerned with everything. He weaves all the events of our lives into his pattern. "We know that in everything God works for good with those who love him" (Rom. 8:28). His love never leaves us.

A little boy of four or five was staying at home with his father while his mother was in the hospital. The boy missed his mother most of all at night when he had to go to bed. He wept. His father drew the little fellow's bed close to his own. Still the boy could not sleep. He asked his father to turn on the light, but the father said no. "Only for a moment, Father! It is so dark!" Again came a firm "No." Then the father heard the boy crying. He reached out and took his son's hand in his own. "Thank you, Father," said the lad. "Now it is light!"

Our situation is like that. Often we are groping in the dark. We beg for an explanation, for an easing of the burden, for light. Nothing happens. But then, yes, something does happen. In everything God is working for good with those that love him. In a way we cannot explain, a hand has reached out to us. A word is spoken. A line from a hymn comes to mind. The darkness disappears, and peace fills the soul.

It seem inexplicable that some believe there is

greater comfort in reckoning with fortuitous circumstances than in reckoning with God. Jesus has told us that nothing happens without God's knowing it; we can trust his word. One day the truth of it shall be revealed.

Reckoning with God is part of the ABC of faith. We must never outgrow practicing it. Taking God with us into all the experiences of life is part of his means of making things work together for good. It is written: "Commit your way to the Lord; trust in him, and he will act" (Ps. 37:5).

God is watching over all;
Holds your hand lest you fall.
In your valley of despair–
Without peace or rest,
Facing trouble's test–
God will yet be there
Watching still,
Shielding from ill,
Till you reach the end of sorrow
In a blessed, calm tomorrow.

E. Stockmann

7

Don't Be Afraid

Fear as to what life may bring is plaguing the people of our time. In spite of the increase in knowledge and the great strides being taken in science, people today are afraid.

Throughout the world a sigh is borne,
A sigh the world—perplexed, forlorn—
Cannot explain. With sudden smart
How shrill it swells and seems to soar,
Then pierces keen the soul's sick core
And the lonely fear-struck heart!

TH. W. OLDENBURG

In fact, men have been afraid ever since the day the cherubim with flaming swords were ordered to guard the gates of paradise. Today it takes more than tranquilizers to drive men's fears away.

Has life really any meaning? Will the tangled threads somewhere be straightened and woven together? How do we find peace of mind? Where do we find strength to bear our burdens? We cling to life, and yet we are afraid of it. Afraid of the future. Afraid of death. Afraid of judgment. Afraid of ourselves. Life has become too complicated, and evils follow at the heels of progress. Is it any wonder that we are perplexed and insecure?

No, it is not strange. But it is imperative for us to

learn the nature of this anxiety and discover the possibilities of overcoming it.

Why does anxiety rob us of our strength? It is because of sin. Anxiety is a symptom which shows that there is something the matter with us. What are we really anxious about? Are we concerned about what produces evil, or about that which *is* evil? As soon as we ask this question, we discover what is wrong. The truth is that we fear what hurts us more than we fear evil itself. We are confused. The real danger is buried so deep within us that we do not fear most what is most harmful.

Luther begins his exposition of the Ten Commandments with the words, "We should fear and love God so that . . ." The words "fear and love God" sound strange to our ears because we have forgotten that the fear of God is the beginning of wisdom. He who truly fears God has trust and confidence. He has the assurance that God has established his household on earth and that whatever God wills is right.

Fear of the future, or fear of God? The choice should not be difficult. Yet it is as hard for us as it was for the disciples. They had lived with Jesus. They had been present when he performed his miracles. They had heard him say to Jairus after his daughter's death, "Fear not. Just believe!" They had been told whom they should fear and what they should not fear. Nonetheless it was hard for them to put knowledge into action. To the very last Jesus tried to show them the right way. "Let not your hearts be troubled;

you believe in God, believe also in me" (John 14:1). But they failed.

The real problem is not how to get rid of anxiety, but how to let Christ have more power within us. No one on earth has the right to say with authority, "You need not be afraid." We are all afraid.

Only One has both the right and the power to banish anxiety—Jesus Christ. The closer we live to him day by day, the greater strength we shall have to stand fast when evil times come. When Christ stands between us and our fears, we have peace in our hearts. And when we have this peace, we can endure much.

Shepherd kind, our source of gladness,
Your sweet name
In every pain
Quiets our hearts' sadness!
Savior, Lord, before your throne,
There shall we
In harmony
Make our thanksgiving known.

PAUL GERHARDT

8

In Our Father's Hands

"Our Father who art in heaven . . ." We learned these words when we were very young. Indeed one of the first things we learned about God is that he is our Father. That is good! Since God is our Father, we can be sure that he cares for us.

We are not left to fend for ourselves, and life is not just an accident. Everything rests in the hands of our heavenly Father. We are in good hands. All the threads of life, including the dark ones, are woven into a pattern, for our Father knows what we need. We feel secure when we accept this truth.

We are not guessing about it. When we say that we believe in God the Father Almighty, we are not speaking empty words. We have learned this expression from our Lord Jesus Christ, and he does not deceive us. He pointed to the birds of the air and to the lilies of the field. "Notice how God cares for them," he said. Doesn't he care much more for you? Talk with your Father! God knows all your needs, and he cares for you.

Since God is our Father, we may turn to him to ask for forgiveness.

Some of us remember how Father and Mother said, "You must ask forgiveness!" It was humiliating to confess our mistakes and to ask for forgiveness. But how good it was to be forgiven! All the world seemed different, and we could breathe freely again.

Jesus said that our heavenly Father will treat us in the same way. Go to him and make full confession. Have confidence in your Father and ask his forgiveness!

"Father, I have sinned!" said the prodigal son when he returned. He was received without reservations. His father met him with open arms. God is like that. He is *our* Father.

Since God is our Father, whatever he does will be for our good.

We do not always agree with him as to what is best for us. But he makes no mistakes. Since he sent Jesus to earth to save us, we can trust him for everything we need. We may talk to him about anything. Nothing is too big, nothing too small. He does not weary of listening. He is concerned for our welfare. And he is all powerful.

Since God is our Father, we always have a place of refuge.

Life is not easy, and we must confess that no one understands us fully. We try to explain our problems, but no one can help us with them. Others cannot appreciate our greatest needs. But God understands. He does not explain all the riddles of life, but he understands.

In our childhood we often fled to Mother or Father when we were distressed and fearful. When Father took us in his arms and told us that all would be well with us, we could easily do without explanations. It gave us confidence when Father assured us that he understood us and that he could and would help us.

So it is with God. He is our Father who knows us and cares for us. We can always rely on him.

He who has helped me hitherto
Will be my help forever.
His grace to me each morn is new,
His mercy ceases never.
All things are spread before his eyes;
In love he hears his children's cries,
His care on them bestowing.

GRUNDTVIG

9

Our Lord Knows the Way

"One path or another," we sing, "our Lord knows the way." Well, it is easy to sing, but not so easy to believe when a storm breaks over us. It is a good thing that our Bible is an honest book, showing us how men have had to struggle to keep their faith.

Why is it so hard to believe that our Lord does know the way?

One reason is that this world is in the hands of the evil one. Some people think that this statement is too pessimistic. It isn't. The power of evil is not to be underestimated. Think of your own experiences! Why is it so easy to do wrong and so hard to do right? Why do we go down to defeat in this struggle? "For I do not do the good I want, but the evil I do not want is what I do" (Rom. 7:19).

Why?

The whole world is in the power of the evil one, and that evil is much stronger and much more evil than we want to admit. How cruel, for example, men are to their fellow men! How we embitter their lives! And we Christians are not without blame. We need not look to the world at large to find evidence of it. We need only look at ourselves.

It sometimes seems that God is unconcerned about the evils and the suffering in the world. Why doesn't he intervene? Why doesn't he prove that ultimate power and might are his? This question bothers us every once in a while.

Well, yes, God is passive at times. And that means suffering. Being passive means both suffering and compassion. Rightly understood, there is a reason when he does not act. If we cannot see it anywhere else, we see it with Jesus on the cross at Golgotha. Why didn't God have the lightning strike? Why didn't he send twelve legions of angels to sweep aside Caiaphas and Pilate and their aides? God did not act. But in the suffering of Christ the greatest act of all time was accomplished.

God finds the way to ultimate good. But it is up to us to find the right attitude in our own lives. The fact that God can find the way out of difficulties does not mean that we can expect to have all our wishes fulfilled. Often when we pray for God's help, we want him to help us have *our* way. "*Thy* will be done!" we say. But do we pray that prayer whole heartedly?

The Lord knows a way. His ways are past finding out, but they are never without reason; and he who dares to trust in God will one day discover that in the end God's ways are always best.

What is the difference between faith and resignation? That can, perhaps, be best answered in this way: resignation is giving up or letting go; faith is giving oneself to someone or something. In faith there is a confidence that enables one to give himself to others. In resignation there is only weakness, disappointment, and perhaps bitterness. In a word, the difference between faith and resignation is *obedience.*

When we say, "Somehow or other, the Lord will find a way," we show that we are not forgetting that evil will always lose the last round. How can we know that? We know it because Jesus said so. We know it because there was an Easter. "We know for sure that he has lost who went with God to battle."

But how do we gain such assurance? It comes when we let the Word of God prevail over us. Then the question is reversed. Now it is God who asks and we who must answer. "Do you believe in me?" asks the Lord. "Do you think well of me? Do you believe in my invincible power and my blessed purpose? Do you believe in me enough to let me rule?"

How shall we answer him?

Where God leads me I find faith
And hope and a quiet heart;
And his own strength then dwells in me—
What ever could force us apart?
I cling to his hand with fervent trust
Because God's way is always just—
The best, I know from the start.

BRORSON

10

Help Is at Hand

Many years ago I was chaplain at St. Luke's hospital in Hellerup, making my daily rounds among the sick, having devotions with them, and talking with each about his greatest need. It was a difficult but enriching experience, constantly reminding one of how weak a man is in his own strength.

As I stood at the door of a sick-room, I often asked myself, "How much do you dare to promise this patient?" You have come to bring the Gospel of Jesus Christ. But how much of the Gospel can you tell the very sick?

You can quote some favorite passages from the Scriptures: "Call upon me in the day of trouble; I will deliver thee, and thou shalt glorify me" (Ps. 50:15, KJV); or "Commit thy way unto the Lord; trust also in him" (Ps. 37:5, KJ); or "Cast thy burden upon the Lord, and he shall sustain thee" (Ps. 55:22a, KJ). Such passages you can quote easily; but if a patient asks you if they mean that anyone who believes in God will be helped, or healed, how will you answer him?

The truth is that we will have *help,* but we want it to be physical help. It is good to hear about salvation, a man may say, but physical help is what we need, especially in the midst of sickness and sorrow.

God must help us; if he cannot or will not, what good is he to us?

Even though we hate to admit it, there are times when it is hard for us to be satisfied with Christ's gospel of salvation. It is hard sometimes to be content as Paul was when—in spite of his prayers—the "thorn in his flesh" was not taken away. Paul could still profess his faith: "The Lord said to me, 'My grace is sufficient for thee'" (2 Cor. 12:9, KJ). And Paul was satisfied.

The distance between us and God is sometimes so great that we think physical help is more important than salvation. We want God's gifts and benefits, but *the Gift,* God's unspeakable gift, seems of secondary importance. We want to use God to promote our aims and to fulfill our desires. We want him to perform miracles and grant us temporal relief. What we are saying is, we'll give God our faith if he will just do what we want him to.

But we are on the wrong track. It is right for us to talk with God about all things, especially about our troubles and anxieties. It is also true that God does intervene. There is no use in praying if we do not believe that miracles can happen. All true prayer is marked by confidence in God's power and good will. We believe that true prayer can set forces in motion to bring about outcomes that would not otherwise develop or to prevent actions that could not otherwise be stopped. This is all quite true.

Then what is the problem? Merely that we are

wrong if we want to use God just as a means of fulfilling our physical or material desires. It is wrong if we forget the one thing needful, if we forget that the salvation of our souls is more important than our temporal needs.

Help is at hand. We must never doubt it. But help comes to us through Jesus Christ. It does not come in surprise packages or in letters with money enclosed. It comes in the Word that God has given us. He does not promise relief and ease; he does promise deliverance and salvation. Faith in Christ does not promise worldly success, but it does give us God's promises to be with us all the way.

His help is at hand. But if we are to receive it, we must understand God's purposes and try living in accordance with them. We are apt to grow tired and impatient when others do not agree with us. We insist on being right, on having our own way. But the person who always insists on his rights cuts himself off from God's help.

If God is to speak to us, we must be ready to listen to him. The hard roads often prove to be God's shortcuts to human hearts. Once we make the right turn, we learn from our hardships to value what is really right.

Help is at hand. But we must remember, too, that the way of Jesus is the way of the cross. He suffered so that we might know we are never alone. He is always going before us. He keeps saying, "Follow me!" He will bring us safely home.

Rejoice then, ye sad-hearted,
Who sit in deepest gloom,
Who mourn o'er joys departed,
And tremble at your doom:
He who alone can cheer you
Is standing at the door;
He brings his pity near you,
And bids you weep no more.

PAUL GERHARDT

11

Under His Wings

It is good to be indoors on an autumn day when the wind is howling through the trees, and dry leaves swirl through the air as they fall to the ground. Some think that autumn is beautiful. I confess that I am not one of them. The rich colors of the trees, vines, and fall flowers do not deceive me. I am facing the reality that everything fades away and dies. Just as the flowers on the casket cannot hide the horror of death, no more can a beautiful September day deny the truth that winter is on its way.

Fall forces sober reflection. Three things never return—so we read in our school books as children—the arrow shot from the bow, the word once spoken, and time gone by. Our footprints are behind us; a reckoning is before us; only today is ours. More than this we know not. How does all this affect our lives? Are we safe inside the door? Do we realize what it means to have found a shelter? These are autumn thoughts.

Jonas Lie in the last half of the nineteenth century wrote a letter to Bjørnstjerne Bjørnson, saying that he thought death must be a natural closing of life, as natural as the falling of leaves in the autumn. "But something kept whispering within me. It was my spirit which wanted more, much more." The urge led him to find Christ in God's Word. "The day when my eyes found him was the happiest day of my life." True enough! For where Christ is, there is no autumn.

We do have to find shelter. But where do we look for it?

To have shelter, we must first realize that forgiveness and restitution are available. Jesus did not say to the lame man at Capernaum just, "Be of good cheer, for I will make you whole!" That would not have been enough. He said, "Be of good cheer; your sins are forgiven."

Jesus came into this world so that we could find a place of safety. He gave us the name of God the Father to call on and taught us that all things rest in the hands of the Father. He came to restore the relation between God and lost mankind, teaching us that salvation first of all has to do with the forgiveness of sins. So in Holy Communion we speak these words: "This cup is the new testament in my blood which is shed for you for the remission of sins" (Matt. 26:28, KJV). Here is the core of the Gospel. Finding shelter begins with obtaining God's forgiveness.

The door is open, and we do not need to stand outside in the cold. When we were children, Mother taught us to pray an evening prayer: "O Father in heaven, keep us in thy loving care." We did not understand it fully, but we have not forgotten the words. The older we grow, the better we know how necessary it is to find a safe refuge in God's protection.

As a young pastor I once conducted the funeral service for a young blacksmith. He had been big and strong, a man of few words, but straight and genuine. His mother was a widow, and he was her comfort. In his illness when the ambulance came for him, he said, "Mother, I should like to live, for your sake; therefore we shall pray to God that it may be so. But if I am not permitted to return, you must not grieve too much. You know that I can safely leave this world and that Jesus will save me." He did not return, but he left this world in peace. He knew what it meant to be under the wings of his heavenly Father.

It is good to be safe in God's care, not only when we come to die, but also because life itself is difficult, and our enemy is strong. If we learn to live, dying will take care of itself. It is living each day that concerns us. Today we must have a place of shelter. Today we must go to God in Jesus' name. Today we must pray that we may abide in the shelter of his wings. Let the storm rage and the darkness deepen! It is still true that if we dwell with God, all is well with our souls.

In Psalm 32 where we are told of the importance of finding shelter and safety, and where the truth is emphasized that this can only come if we confess our sins and receive God's forgiveness, we read, "Thou art my hiding place; thou shalt preserve me from trouble; thou shalt compass me about with songs of deliverance. . . . He that trusteth in the Lord, mercy shall compass him about" (Ps. 32:7, 10, KJ). Praise be to God that these words are true.

Then rest, my soul, without a care
On Jesus' breast at peace!
Let pleasures never tempt you there,
Rejoicing until death's release
That God through Christ has chosen you.
Your tears dispelled, your faith anew
Shows how he measures out your way!
Oh, let glad trust in him relieve you,
Know God himself will not deceive you;
Rest in his peace from day to day.

BRORSON

12

The Finest Word

Bishop Berggrav, toward the end of his life, spoke over the radio on the subject, "What Life Has Taught Me." Among other things, he said, "Life taught me early that its best things are undeserved and that one word which I did not care about in my youth—the word *grace*—is the finest and most important word of all."

Why is *grace* the finest word of all?

It is because grace blots out all my sins. As we erase a problem from the blackboard after struggling with it, so God, in the name of Jesus, erases our debts to him. We are baptized into this faith. In the baptismal ritual, we hear the words: "The almighty God, the Father of our Lord, Jesus Christ, who hath begotten thee again of water and the Holy Ghost, and hath forgiven thee all thy sins, strengthen thee with his grace unto life everlasting." Grace is the finest word because it blots out all my sins.

Grace sets new forces in motion. "Be strong in the grace that is in Christ Jesus!" (2 Tim. 2:1) says Paul to a good friend and co-laborer. Grace is an active word. The people who think grace is a pillow on which to sleep are wrong. We cannot take our ease in the confidence that all will be well because God will have mercy on us. A call goes out from grace for us to fight against sin. Yet if we live under grace, we shall have victory over the power of sin.

Søren Kierkegaard said that Christianity consists of three things: "unending humiliation–and thus grace–and thus the strivings of gratitude [grateful hearts]." The three belong together. Gratitude's strivings after we have been freed from sin drive us back to perpetual humiliation, where we again find the need for grace to blot out sin–and then we begin once more with the strivings of gratitude. This is the rhythm of the Christian's daily life.

Why is grace the finest word? Because it enables me to stand in the great day [of judgment].

Berggrav, during his last Christmas season, wrote a letter to the first congregation he had served as a young man. He ends the letter with these words:

"And so I am sitting in my easy chair, not knowing whether this is my last Christmas. There is nothing sad about the thought. An old man with a life full of weeds and wounds–unbelievable as it sounds –has had imputed to him, by God, that which his Redeemer has done for him, and is graciously accepted as a child of God. This is what Christmas is–that God came to earth and took upon himself the condition of men so that we may attain to his [condition]. In the eyes of God both Eva [his little granddaughter] and I are angels now. This is not to be fathomed. But it is to be *believed.*

"United in this faith we greet one another with wishes for a Christmas of joy!"

Thus wrote a man for whom grace was the finest word.

"By the grace of God I am what I am" (1 Cor. 15:10), says Paul. And that is not an empty phrase. Where can I hide if I cannot believe that the Lord will let the light of his countenance shine upon me and give me peace? How can I struggle bravely if I cannot believe that God in his grace is renewing my strength as I go? How can I stand in the day of judgment if God in his grace will not help me? "By the grace of God I am what I am."

"Christianity is God's word of grace," we read in one of our hymns. It means that there will be an open door on that day [of judgment]. Enter that door while there is still time. Do not try to do this or that first. Come as you are, trusting in God's grace. His grace is sufficient for you.

Oh, God be praised for thy word of grace
To comfort us in sorrow!
And God be praised for Jesus' steps
Which the little ones can follow!
And God be praised for thy Spirit Holy,
A guiding power for meek and lowly
To heaven's bright tomorrow.

GRUNDTVIG

13

From Day to Day

About six sevenths of the days of our life are week days. It is therefore most important to consider how we live these days. How do we take what comes to us each day? How do we value our time? How do we go about rating our days as plus or minus? What are our usual habits of living and thinking? What is most characteristic of our daily life?

When Jesus Christ spoke about the last day, he said, "The Son of Man is to come with his angels in the glory of his Father, and then he will repay every man for what he has done" (Matt. 16:27). The Greek word for work is *praxis*. On that day God will speak to us about our *praxis*, our work.

Perhaps you grow fearful as you think of this verse. We must confess that we are apt to sort life's affairs into two bags. In one bag are our everyday problems and difficulties—everything we struggle with at home or work. In the other bag is our faith, and that bag is far from full. It is not strange, then, that fear strikes and life seems to fall apart when we realize that we are to be judged according to our work.

Yesterday will never return. We know nothing about tomorrow. Today is our day. Today we must show to whom we belong and whom we serve. Faith is concerned with today. It is useless to worry about tomorrow, and it is futile to keep saying "There was a time . . ." Today we have our rendezvous with destiny. Today we must show whether or not we can endure.

Some will say that it is impossible not to worry about the future, adding that it is not wise to be unconcerned about life.

True, we should order the affairs of life to the best of our ability, and it is certainly our duty to take precautions for our welfare and the welfare of our fellow men. There is no argument here.

But that is different from being troubled and careworn about many things. What, we say, if something terrible should happen. Shall I be able to hold out, to stand fast? It is a useless question. Cares and troubles come to all of us in due course, but we never receive the strength today to carry tomorrow's burdens. What is to be gained by being anxious about tomorrow? Nothing but a downcast spirit to rob us of the joy of today.

A song often heard on one radio program begins, "Only a day, only a moment . . ." Why are there so many requests for that song? Perhaps because people have the feeling that it says something important, something that we need to hear. "The burdens of the day he will carry." Yes, he will. Then we do not need to nurse any unnecessary cares.

"Give us *this day* our daily bread," we ask in the Lord's Prayer. Jesus purposely worded the petition this way. God will give us what we need this day.

Then we can give God our declaration of confidence that he will not fail us.

"Praise God! From day to day he bears our burdens." These words reflect the thoughts of a psalm from the Old Testament. How much more we should rejoice who have learned from Jesus Christ that God cares for us! From day to day he will be near us. From day to day we may knock at his door and find that our God is rich enough to help all who call upon him. He will bear our griefs from day to day.

But to return to the question of our daily work—we must remember that our work is the subject that God will talk to us about on the last day. There are a few things that we can all be agreed upon, no matter how different our circumstances may be.

First of all, we have much to be thankful for, and we must never forget to show our gratitude to God. In one hymn we sing of the "thousand blessings" he showers upon us. If you begin to count your blessings, you will find that they cannot be numbered.

Then, the knowledge that God has helped us in the past gives us confidence to say, "Praise the Lord who bears our burdens from day to day." With confidence in him, we can walk fearlessly each day.

And finally, the more we become concerned in our daily work with the question of how we shall be saved, the more help we shall receive for each day's tasks. Think big about the biggest! Then you will be able to think straight about everything else.

Like God's little children here below
Keep close to him, wherever you go!
Ask from your Father power and love,
And rest in his peace from heaven above.
Oh, God be praised!

GRUNDTVIG

14

With His Blessing

"God bless you, my boy!" Thus has many a mother and father bid farewell to a child as he was about to fare forth into a perilous world. There is no finer farewell gift than God's blessing.

But what does it mean? What does the blessing signify? "He lifted up his hands and blessed them" (Luke 24:50). These are the last words we read from the lips of Jesus. It happened on Ascension Day, near Bethany. He blessed his disciples. He did the same thing when the little children were brought to him. He laid his hands on them and blessed them. What does that mean?

We come upon the word *blessing* again and again in the Old Testament. When Abraham was told to set forth on an unknown journey, God said to him, "I will bless you . . . so that you will be a blessing" (Gen. 12:2). When Jacob's nightlong struggle ended, he was granted an answer to his plea, "I will not let you go unless you bless me" (Gen. 32:26). And we read, "And there he blessed him" (Gen. 32:29c). Aaron, the first high priest, blessed the Israelites with the same words which are heard in our own church services to this day:

The Lord bless you and keep you;
The Lord make his face to shine upon you;
The Lord lift up his countenance upon
you, and give you peace.
(Num. 6:24-26)

The word that is used for *blessing* in the Hebrew of the Old Testament means the *communication of vital power.* To be blessed, then, means to receive that strength which enables a person to accept well whatever happens to him. It enables one to stand the test when puzzling or difficult problems confront him. It helps one to understand the purpose of life. Much more is inherent in the term, but essentially, blessings bring strength from above for living a right life. Without it a person may win riches and power and honor. But without the blessing of God, life's real purposes cannot be achieved. What then is the good of all the rest?

The prayer that is used when a bridal couple kneels at the altar petitions the Lord for three gifts: grace, happiness, and blessing. Happiness alone is not enough. It must be girded by grace and blessing before its whole meaning can be fulfilled. Dear Lord, let this all come to pass!

A blessing must be accepted with childlike confidence. Critics and skeptics may act like Esau, who sold his birthright for a bowl of lentils. Those who do not believe can have no part in the blessings of the Lord. The great danger of our time lies in the fact that since men are learning to unlock the secrets of the universe, simple faith is having its most difficult struggle to survive.

Let us by all means make use of our intelligence. It is no sign of piety for a man to accept uncritically everything that is presented to him in the name of knowledge.

As one wise man has said, the calamity of our time is not that there is too much thinking, but that there is too little. Our views of life are inclined to be set by slogans and maxims without our taking time to think much about them.

Let us also remember that the greatest things in life are usually the simple things and that he who has lost a childlike confidence in divine guidance does not have much left, no matter how great his knowledge.

Our Father in heaven,
Let me now be given
Contentment and light,
That lifelong I may be
Led like a child by thee,
With simple faith in thy great might.

With these words Mathias Claudius lifts an evening prayer expressing an elementary condition for experiencing the blessing of the Lord.

Some people seem to have everything their hearts desire. It may not be so. If God's blessing is missing, no heart can be satisfied. Blessing and long life belong together. Without blessing, the heart has no peace.

Take the blessing of the Lord into your reckoning. It may help you to see some things you have missed. It may help you to find some things you have lost. God's desire is to bless and protect. Always.

We too can say to him, "Lord, I will not let you go unless you bless me."

God, lay thy hand on mine
And to me give
Thy Holy Ghost divine
With me to live.
Bless me, Lord God, from heaven's wondrous height!
Grant me each day and hour,
Content, to find the power
To live aright!

KINGO

15

The Canceled Debt

Certain questions seem common to all men in all times. Why am I here? How can I find peace of mind? Where am I going when I am through with this life? Everyone knows that such questions arise and that it is not good to suppress them.

How do I know that there is a merciful God? This is another question common among men. Many religions have tried to answer it. Men have tried in vain to assure themselves of God's good will by attempts at moral self-improvement, by good deeds, by self-torture, by meditation. But such methods are futile.

How can anyone be sure that there is a merciful God? The answer comes in Christianity's message of salvation for men through Jesus Christ. Hear how Paul expresses it: "Who shall bring any charge against God's elect? It is God who justifies. Who is to condemn? Is it Jesus Christ who died, yes, who was raised from the dead, who is at the right hand of God, who indeed intercedes for us" (Rom. 8:33, 34)? Or in another passage, " . . . having canceled the bond which stood against us, with its legal demands; this he set aside, nailing it to the cross" (Col. 2:14).

God is the one who justifies us; our salvation rests

upon this belief. But what does that mean—to say that God justifies us?

A professor of theology once said, "If somebody were to ask me why I became a Christian, I would think about it and probably weep when I gave the answer. I would have to say, 'Because I have to have forgiveness.'" It's a good answer. Christianity is the religion that preaches that God is the one who justifies us.

Justification is the same as pardon. It is useless to ask how we can think of God as one who will pardon us for the sake of Jesus. It cannot really be understood. It can only be believed. But Jesus has told us the story of the publican who said, "God be merciful to me a sinner . . . this man went down to his house justified" (Luke 18:13). He received the mercy he had asked for.

Christianity is the religion of the canceled debt. No one is shut out because of the number of his sins. The only thing that can shut a man off from God's mercy is his own disbelief. If I will not accept God's offer of forgiveness in repentance and prayer, in faith and thanksgiving, the blame is mine and the responsibility for it.

God's forgiveness is something different from pardon through punishment. When a mother forgives her child, the wrong-doing is canceled on earth. And yet—. The mother will now be particularly careful with the child in situations like the one in which the fault occurred. The genuineness of her forgiveness is shown by her readiness to help the child and to prevent a repetition of the offense. And with the child, the sense of being forgiven should make him try to be more careful in the future. In the forgiveness of sin lies the seed of a good harvest.

The canceled sin is more than a pardon. It is a call to us to strive against sin. Grace always entails responsibility. Jesus taught us that in the Lord's Prayer: "Forgive us our debts, as we also have forgiven our debtors" (Matt. 6:12). Grace should harvest what it sows.

Many years ago I spoke to a group of confirmands about the difference between the work of the high priest under the old covenant and the work of Jesus in the new covenant. A bright young lad said, "The high priest could pay no more than the interest on the debt when he offered the sacrificial lamb on the mercy seat of the Holy of Holies. But Jesus paid up the whole debt, so that it no longer existed." It can hardly be put more clearly.

God be praised for the canceled debt!

I this day have sinned, dear Lord,
Broken laws, against thy Word.
Grant me grace, through Jesus' blood,
Turn my waywardness to good!

LOUISE HENSEL

16

The Gospel of Peace

"Christianity is, in effect, the gospel of peace." But what is meant by peace? "God's peace, which passes all understanding"—what is that (Phil. 4:7)? "God's peace in the house," they said in the old days. God's peace means more than being watched by guardian angels, Grundtvig tells us. What do such words really mean? Are they truth or poetry? "Peace be with you" (John 20:19), said the risen Savior when he met the disciples after his victory over death. "My peace I give to you" (John 14:27), he promised his disciples on his last evening with them, and he kept the promise. But what does it mean? Do we know anything about this gospel of peace?

Peace, in the true meaning of the word, is a condition of living. It is so in a nation, in the home, and in the life of the individual. When there is no peace, life is disturbed and crippled; then it dies. Life and peace cannot be separated. We really live only when we have peace.

The requisite for peace, then, is that we be allied with powers stronger than those that destroy life. It is not enough for us to sigh for peace. In the cemetery there is many a monument on which rests a white dove with an olive leaf staring down at withered flowers and black earth. "Peace" we read on the inscription. Ah yes! But we must not forget the requisites for peace. In the days of the old covenant there were false prophets who preached Peace, peace! when there was no peace. It was vain prophecy.

Peace comes as the result of something else. The New Testament speaks of grace and peace, forgiveness and peace, faith and peace.

In the letter to the Ephesians, Paul says of Christ, "He is our peace" (Eph. 2:14). He has broken down the wall of partition between Jew and Gentile, and —even more important—between man and God. Peace is in him. He makes peace, proclaims peace; and to live within the bounds which his name creates is to have peace with God through his name.

But, you may ask, can a man have a feeling of being at peace with God? Well, how much or little one may feel is dependent upon many things. Feelings are changeable. We can be grateful that we do not have to depend upon our emotions. The gospel does not deal with emotions, but with Jesus Christ who remains faithful in the midst of our inconstancy.

What is of most concern is the relation between faith and peace. Faith is not something that we trade for peace. Nor do we secure peace by good deeds. But our faith establishes a relationship with God which lets God speak to us and proclaim the gospel of peace. Faith has meaning only as it brings us into contact with Jesus Christ. Faith is obedience, evidencing itself by our yielding to Christ's gospel of judgment and forgiveness, truth and grace. "Thy faith hath made thee whole; go in peace" (Mark 5:34; Luke 8:48, KJV), Jesus said to the woman who came to him in her need. He says the same thing today.

We must remember that we live in a world of struggle. There is a close relationship between war and peace. Everyone who lives his daily life with God knows that. The peace of God is not to be found in our snug shelters; it is won in the storm and stress of life.

Our struggles are of many kinds. There is the struggle against one's obstinate self; the struggle to hold one's ground when life goes against him; the effort to bring life's troubles within God's compass and thus to strengthen our faith. "Often full of restlessness, ever full of faith in Christ," says Kingo. Here is the good fight of faith. But the gospel of peace brings a joyous message, urging us to fight with courage, for God will give us the victory through Jesus Christ, our Lord.

Christmas greetings midst storm and strife
Herald peace and joy in life;
Peace above the clash of soul,
Peace to win the final goal;
High in joy or deep in sorrow,
Peace for both today, tomorrow.

HOSTRUP

17

How to Believe

In common speech "believe" is a weak word. "Sure, I believe that," we say, though usually we know little or nothing about it. We just think we believe it at the time.

In the New Testament, "believe" is a strong word. It indicates, not something we believe *that,* but something we believe *in* or *on.* Belief here expresses a personal relationship with someone we can base our faith upon. "Faith," says the New Testament, "is a conviction."

We hear people say, "If I could only believe! If I only had more faith!" They do not know where their road is taking them. Is there something they should be doing about it? Will they be able to feel it when they do believe? How does it all fit together?

In our Christian faith, Jesus is the central figure. He is the pioneer, and we must take our positions in reference to him. He is both the subject and the object of the sentence

Even the most penetrating psychology is unable to describe just what happens when a person begins to believe. But a simple illustration may help us. Suppose someone recommends a man to me as a fine, trustworthy person. It may be so, but I cannot believe it without seeing him. I meet him, and we talk together. If he inspires confidence, something happens while we talk together. When he leaves, I say to myself, there goes a man I can depend upon. I have not done anything at all. It was he who opened the way. That is how faith is established.

So it is in our relationship with Jesus. He is the pioneer of our faith. "Come and see" (John 1:39), Jesus said to the disciples. He made no demands on them, but he extended the invitation. They came, they saw, they remained with him. "We have beheld his glory" (John 1:14), said one of them. Something took place in their life with him, and they came to understand that only in him could their deepest need be satisfied. They were not perfect and could not understand fully, but they were bound to him with the conviction of faith.

In the gospels we meet two persons who Jesus said had great faith: the woman of Cana and the centurion of Capernaum. They were both pagans and had no knowledge as to who Jesus was. But they sought him in their distress and were assured that he could help them. The woman of Cana broke through hindrances to reach him, and the centurion was satisfied to have Jesus speak only a word. A great faith, said Jesus. Faith is the same as trust.

And faith is obedience. It is action, not theory. "Only the obedient believe," a wise man said. That is, if you want to believe, you must do something about it. When Jesus says, "Come," you must come. When he says, "Go into your room and pray" (Matt.

6:6), you must do it. When he shows you the way, you must follow it. "Only the obedient believe." That is true. "Not every one who says to me 'Lord, Lord,' shall enter the kingdom of heaven, but he who does the will of my Father who is in heaven" (Matt. 7: 21). To have faith is to be put in motion on the road of obedience.

We remember what Luther says about the Holy Spirit in his explanation of the third article of the catechism: "I believe that I cannot of my own reason or strength believe in Jesus Christ my Lord, or come to him; but the Holy Ghost has called me through the Gospel." Anyone who really wants to believe must pray for the light and guidance of the Holy Spirit.

By faith we are divinely sure
That grace to us is given.
No human effort can secure
This precious gift from heaven.
'Tis God himself who must begin
The blessed work of faith within
And lead us to the Savior.

BRORSON

18

The Miracle of Returning Life

When we walk through the countryside on a spring day, we see the miracle of life emerging before our eyes. Nature is coming to life. In fields and gardens, in meadows and woods we can see it happen. Spring's sparkling beauty shows how fair the earth is under the working of God's laws. Day by day the sun waxes in strength; everything in nature is growing.

It is the miracle of life renewed; and the larks are singing.

In Christian Richard's spring song, "Welcome Little Lark," we see the happy songster soaring higher, higher until it is only a speck in the sky:

Thou dost not flutter round
But cheerful, gay, from the ground
Dost wing thy dauntless way
Aloft from earth to heaven.

The lines are pretty and true.

They remind us of our own situation. God has granted us the wonderful gift of life. Never forget it. Try singing a song for him, thanking him for the lovely day. Even if the day is not pleasant but overcast and dreary, remember that you still have the wonderful gift of life.

We cannot, like the lark, soar in our own strength from earth to heaven. Whether we like to hear it or not, the Old Testament words are true: "For dust thou art, and unto dust thou shalt return" (Gen. 3: 19, KJV). We ourselves cannot conquer darkness or death.

But the incomprehensible truth is that our Creator is also our Redeemer, and the miracle of eternal life has been proclaimed in a way for all of us to see it. For Christ is risen.

Let us put it another way. In the light of the words of our Lord, we can see a path from earth to heaven. We do not turn first to our own reason for proof that God's Word is true. We turn to Christ, the crucified and risen Savior. His words are spirit and life, and through him we can experience—in spite of sin and death—the wonderful truth that we too can rejoice in the treasure of life. The sword of God's Word may cut us to bits, but the truth is that only those whose hearts have been broken can find the way to heaven.

Let us listen once more to the spring song of the lark. Why does it sing? The poet replies, "Whether soaring or dipping, you are true to your call, and therefore your days are so happy!"

Where there is life, there are laws. To have joy in life, we must accommodate ourselves to them. There is a purpose in life, through light days and dark days; and it is our call to fulfill that purpose. Some find it easier to give up and drift. But aimless ease never brings fulness of life.

The wonder of life is enjoyed only by those who accept living as a divine call to service. "If I within my given place, my God and Father rightly serve," says Kingo in his morning hymn, "accept my call with faithfulness, my days will then be happy." True enough. The forces of life are active when we are obedient and faithful.

One more reference to Christian Richard: he calls the lark the true bird of faith because it appears early when things are just beginning to sprout. It dares to sing before summer has arrived. It is brave. "It heralds on high the gentle breezes of spring."

Faith is like that. It proclaims the wonders of life. It relies on what the Creator and Redeemer of life has said and done. April may be cold and snowy, but summer is on the way. Faith is courageous because it lives on God's sure Word. We have not yet seen all things subject to Christ. We are still in the hour of struggle. We are still subject to death. The powers of darkness rage. But where God's life-giving spirit operates, we are freed from sin and death and then we too, like the lark can "herald from on high the gentle breezes of spring."

Light over the lawn, like a morning in song,
A morning in May, when it's greening!
The power of delight conquers darkness and light,
Even so, God's mercy is streaming!
Songs from the heart at eve or at morn
Echoing deep from each hilltop are borne!

GRUNDTVIG

19

The Full Assurance of Faith

Can faith and assurance be reconciled? When we say about one thing or another, "I think so," there may be some uncertainty in the mind. But the New Testament speaks positively about the full assurance of faith. "Faith is the . . . evidence of things not seen" (Heb. 11:1, KJV).

How does one find the way to complete certainty about faith?

When a natural scientist wants to be sure about something, he experiments in the laboratory. Gradually through these experiments he approaches the answer. His results so far point in one direction, and eventually his tentative hypothesis becomes an established fact.

When a philosopher seeks the truth about some issue, he works with arguments for and against it. With great care the various theories are studied until the philosopher makes some discovery that leads him to the solution.

But personal problems require different methods. If I want to be sure that I can rely on a person, I want to meet him face to face. I cannot be satisfied just by hearing what others are saying about him.

I must make my own decision, even though that involves some risk. Certainty cannot be purchased without its price. I must make my decision and take the risk. I am happy when my choice proves to be right.

John the baptist sent his disciples to Jesus to ask, "Are you he who is to come, or shall we look for another?" (Luke 7:20). He wanted a guaranty that he had made the right choice. But he did not get one. He was told that he must draw his own conclusion based on the evidence at hand.

When the Jews accused Jesus of keeping them in suspense as to who he was, Jesus answered, "I told you, and you do not believe" (John 10:25). The assurance they sought could come only through their own decision with its accompanying risk. We, too, must make our own decision about Christ. Dare we trust him? Do we believe him? Or not?

Complete assurance about our faith is really based upon what God has said and done. We can find no assurance in our own searching for evidence. But God laid a foundation that cannot be shaken. God won for us a victory that is eternally valid. He wants us to know what he has done. He sent us his own Spirit so that we may know what he has done. Through the Holy Spirit comes complete assurance of our faith.

When a ship is being moored, the anchor is cast overboard. Many people have not found full assurance because they are casting their anchors inboard.

How foolish! We must come out of our shells, wrest ourselves free from our own concerns, anchor ourselves in Christ, and let his words guide us.

Grundtvig's hymn for Pentecost tells us how to find assurance in our faith. The Holy Spirit binds together the hearts of earth and heaven. The Spirit assures us that we are God's children. The Spirit leads us in paths of righteousness. If we want to be sure of our faith, we must pray for the guidance of the Holy Spirit.

Because the decision lies with us, faith will always be to some extent a "swinging bridge." Assurance and obedience belong together; where obedience is imperfect, assurance will be imperfect. The bridge is swaying. But the bridge will hold. God has promised it. He is "at work in you, both to will and to work for his good pleasure" (Phil. 2:13); and therefore you can "work out your own salvation with fear and trembling" (Phil. 2:12b). Assurance and obedience are thus united in a life of faith in God.

Jesus, name of wondrous grace,
Fount of mercy and salvation,
First fruit of the new creation,
Weary sinners' resting place,
Banner of the faith victorious,
Anchor of our hope and love,
Guide us in thy footsteps glorious,
Bear us to thy home above.

BRORSON

20

The Indispensable One

A chapter in a biography of Bishop Gabriel Koch tells of the sorrow which came to the bishop when his only son, Christian, died. The young man had been a student of theology at the University of Copenhagen, and the bishop was looking forward eagerly to the day when his son would become a minister in southern Jutland. But that was not to be. As the bishop stood beside his son's casket, he caressed the boy's cheek. "That is from your mother," he said. Then he folded his hands and prayed, "Dear God, now I will say thank you for Christian, and for taking him home to yourself!" In a letter to his daughter he wrote, "We have often, during the last years, prayed that God would help Christian reach his goal. I was thinking particularly about his graduation and entering the ministry. But God had other plans, and we are sure, better ones. It reminds me of what my father once said—that our prayers to God must pass through Jesus, and that from time to time he had to strike out something in them to make them what they ought to be."

Our petitions must pass through Jesus. So, indeed, must our faith and our life. Everything must pass through Jesus. He said, "Apart from me you can do nothing" (John 15:5c). There is a challenge in the words. Some people seem to be getting along very well without faith in Jesus. They live comfortably and enjoy themselves; they earn a lot of money and climb high on the social ladder; they help themselves freely at life's table; and they enjoy themselves. "Don't talk to us about Jesus' being indispensable," they might be saying. Well, they do not have to listen; but they cannot alter the truth. The verse just quoted is from the passage in John where Jesus is speaking about bearing fruit, and the truth remains that if our purpose in life is to be fulfilled, Christ is indispensable.

He alone has power to grant forgiveness. Without forgiveness we can have no peace with God. Without forgiveness there is no peace with one's conscience. Without forgiveness there is no hope.

Moreover, Jesus is indispensable because he alone can bring us within the bounds of God's love. And there we must be if we are to live without fear. There we must dwell if life is to be happy. We cannot stay outside the fold without becoming the prey of the wolf.

Finally, Jesus is indispensable because he alone can help us come through. We sometimes say that we can "never get over" something that has happened to us. Perhaps not. Time does not heal all wounds. But it is comforting to know that we *can get through* some things that we *can't get over*. We cannot make it alone, but Jesus can help us through. Bishop Koch is one who has given trustworthy witness to this truth.

The Bible is a realistic book; it has much to say about the vicissitudes and sufferings of life. Paul mentions some of them. He speaks from experience, and we do well to listen to his words. He mentions tribulations and distress, persecutions and famine, nakedness and peril. Then come these words: "No, in all these things we are more than conquerors through him who loved us" (Rom. 8:37).

It is hard to say what Paul means by the words "more than conquerors." Why isn't he satisfied just to say *conquerors*? *More* than conquerors—what does that mean? Does he mean that God can help us pass through perilous times without our souls' being harmed? Is he thinking of the lessons of life which are learned in hours of darkness? Perhaps.

But one thing is sure. Jesus is indispensable to us if we are to conquer. *With him* who loved us, we are more than conquerors!

He has made it possible for us to become rooted in the love of God. Paul is certain that nothing, absolutely nothing, can separate us from the love of God in Christ. It may be that he must strike out parts of our prayers, but it is absolutely certain that he will help us through whatever comes, even in the days when we can see no way out.

And so you must not despair when darkness comes. You must not ask, "What have I done to be punished so?" You must not let your hands drop in resignation. You must come *through* the difficulty. You will not be alone in your trials. He who has also been tested and has suffered, even Jesus himself, will be at your side. He is the indispensable one. And he is unconquerable.

Jesus, my guide,
Be at my side
Power and grace to provide me;
Thy Spirit, whole,
Breathe through my soul,
Safe now, since thou art beside me!

P. J. Korsholm

21

By the Light of the Word

"We have found a guiding star which we follow from afar, till we come to . . ." Ah yes, till we come to what? Many bright stars have arisen through the course of time, thanks to the progress of science and culture. Great names which history remembers for important findings to benefit mankind deserve appreciation. But these "stars" of earth have one thing in common—they dim or go out when clouds gather.

As we reach that point in life when we begin to wonder which is the right course to take, we are likely to feel pretty much in the dark. It is not within the scope of science to point out the goals of life. Where shall we go for answers to the deep, burning questions?

"We have found a guiding star . . ." What kind of star? One philosopher has said that the stars of heaven fill him with wonder. That is not strange. What is it that the Bible says? "When I consider thy heavens, the work of thy fingers, the moon and the stars which thou hast ordained; what is man that thou art mindful of him? and the son of man that thou visitest him?" (Ps. 8:3, 4, KJV). Who I am? A speck of dust in the vast universe. Who am I? A creature who is under the care of God, the Almighty. So little am I; yet so great!

Yet the stars themselves cannot give the answer to what we want to know. The stars are distant and silent, and when clouds come their light fades.

"We have found a guiding star." Some can sing it. But many have not found this star. They do not know where to look, and so they wander aimlessly.

The true guiding star is the *Word of God.* "Thy word is a lamp to my feet and a light to my path" (Ps. 119:105).

Just what is the Word of God? It is not a collection of writings from the days of the old covenant and the new. The Word of God is Jesus Christ, our living Lord and Savior. He has brought us the word from God; he himself is the Word of God. And through him we find God.

Christ is the center. The Old Testament points to him; the New Testament reveals him. He is at the center, and as we follow the guiding star through God's Word, we come to Jesus Christ. From him streams the light, and the darkness shall never put it out. (See John 1:1-5.)

There are the laws of time and the laws of the world, but behind and above these laws is the hand of God. Our times are in his hand. All things are in the hands of our heavenly Father.

No one could make such a statement by himself. No one could even think of it by himself. Neither the stars of heaven or the shining stars among mankind could make us believe it is true. There is only one who can do it—Jesus Christ, who himself revealed God's plan for our salvation and who bore all our sins upon the cross. He can convince us that our Father cares for us.

There are those who say that they do not get much out of reading the Bible. They protest that the Word does not *say* anything to them, and that most of what they read they cannot understand. The Bible seems a difficult, complicated book, so they leave it on the shelf.

It isn't true that the four Gospels in the New Testament cannot be understood. Much of what it teaches we learned as children in our Bible study classes. Yet we shall never be done with the study of the Gospels. In their pages we meet Jesus himself. Make it a practice to read something every day from one of the Gospels! You will find food there for your souls.

And how fine it is that we have our hymnbook! Popular songs die, but these hymns are imperishable. In them we have a guiding light to lead us to Jesus Christ.

Neither the Bible nor the hymn book can give an answer to all the questions we can ask, but both show us what we need to know most of all—that the real answers are found in Jesus. He is the way, the truth, and the light.

Our Father, thanks for what we find
Within thy worship holy,
And for thy Spirit, gentle, kind,
To be our guidance solely!
Oh, lead us on by thy Word's dear light
In a life of faith, till upon our sight
Streams the light of heaven's glory!

TH. W. OLDENBURG

22

He Can Fully Save

A group of men were standing one day talking about the church and Christianity. Opinions were divided, and many sharp, contemptuous words were spoken. In the course of the conversation, one of the men said, "People sometimes get too personal about religion. When our girl came home from school the other day, she told us that the teacher had asked her if she believed in Jesus. She had answered that she would go home and ask her mother about it. When the teacher asked why she would have to talk to her mother, our girl replied, 'Well, if my mother doesn't believe in it, it is no good.' "

True, that was a personal question. Religion must become a personal issue, because faith is the most personal relationship in the world. How would you answer if the question were put to you, "Do you believe in Jesus?"

Would you try to evade the question? Many evasive answers have been given. Yes, I believe that there is a life after death. Or, I believe that I shall reach a happy place sometime. Or, I believe that Christianity gives the most exalted view of life. Or, I believe that if we do the best we can, the Lord will do the rest! Do such statements reflect the tone of your answer?

Notice that such replies have one thing in common, the words, "I believe *that*—" But the question was not put that way. The question was, "Do you believe *in* Jesus?" There is a difference between believing *that* and believing *in*. When it is a question of believing *in*, I am completely committed and cannot be satisfied with impersonal suppositions and opinions. I may believe *that* Christian IV died in 1648, but that conviction has no important influence on my life. I believe *in* Jesus Christ, God's only begotten Son, our Lord. If my statement is true, I have been taken captive by Christ, and my conviction will influence my whole life. So we must be careful how we answer. As one man has said, "Do not ask me *if* I believe, but ask me *in whom* I believe." In the final analysis, it is not the strength of my faith that matters, but the strength of the one in whom I put my trust—one who will remain faithful even when I am unfaithful.

"Please reply," so our invitations read. The same request comes with the most important of all invitations: Please reply. It is the invitation itself, however, that concerns us most. It is God's "Yes" to us that saves us. All the promises of God are gathered into one great "Yes," and Jesus has given us this Yes. It is not a yes-and-no answer, but a clear unequivocal affirmative. This reply can bring us home saved.

Listen to what the letter to the Hebrews has to say about Jesus: "Consequently he is able for all time to save those who draw near to God through him, since he always lives to make intercession for them" (Heb. 7:25). This is a good, strong statement.

"To save for all time." Nothing needs to be added. Jesus has taken the matter into his own hands, and he will complete the good work which he has begun. He does not stop halfway, but finishes the work completely. "To the uttermost" is the phrasing of the King James Version.

"To the uttermost." We are in error if we think that what God has given us is merely an extension of something we already had. No, God is not adding to what is ours. He clears the ground and builds on a new foundation. Our good works, our attempts to improve ourselves, our noble strivings, our religious opinions—none of these can save us. God starts along an entirely new line. He says No to our efforts, but a clear strong Yes to the debt that Jesus paid for us. Jesus can save to the uttermost those who come to God *through* him. *Through him.* There is no other way.

"To the uttermost." Jesus saves us from both the guilt of sin and the power of sin. We can believe him when he says that he will make us free indeed.

Evil by nature, and dead in transgression,
Cold as a statue, and hard as a stone,
This was our state when thou, mov'd by compassion,
Chose in thy wisdom to call us thine own.
Led by thy Spirit, and call'd by thy favor,
Heard we the life-giving voice of our Savior.
Halleluja, Halleluja!

BRORSON

23

Signs of Sunrise

A sunrise, when we have the chance to see one, is splendid and overwhelming. First in the eastern sky is a subtle play of shifting colors. Minute by minute the hues change. Then comes the sun. "Sky and sea burst into flaming beauty." Everything is transformed; a new day is born and the birds are all singing together.

Zechariah's song of praise speaks of the blessing of light: "Blessed be the Lord God of Israel; for he has visited and redeemed his people . . . to give light to those that sit in darkness and in the shadow of death, to guide our feet into the way of peace" (Luke 1:68, 79).

"Thanks be to our God for his infinite compassion." These lines of praise stir our wonder. Why did God tolerate for so long his obstinate people in the days of the old covenant? Why didn't he cast them aside and begin anew as the potter did with the clay? Why did God continue to speak through his prophets, so many times in so many ways?

Why did he send Jesus to the lost human race? Why was Jesus given over to die? Why did Easter morning come? There is just one answer to all these questions—it is God's infinite compassion.

He who lets the sun rise upon the evil and the

good really did make a new beginning when he took into his own hands all that belongs to our salvation. He did it because he is the Father of mercy and the God of all comfort.

In a Christmas hymn, Brorson tells why Jesus left his home in heaven in accordance with his Father's will:

'Twas sad for him to think, above,
How we must suffer, so in love
He sought our pain to borrow;
He came to us on earth below,
His mercy great, his heart aglow,
To soothe and heal our sorrow.

That is how it happened. From Christ the light broke forth. Now it is shining for all of us living in darkness under the shadow of death.

But how does a man find the light? A minister once said, "If anyone were to ask me how it is possible to believe in God, I would reply that it is like opening the blinds and letting the sunlight in to fill the room. If we are sitting in darkness, spiritually speaking, it is because we have not let God's sun shine into the room."

No one can answer such questions as these: Is it the sun that makes the flowers open? Or do the flowers open themselves to the sun? No one can tell how it happens that the sunrise comes to us from above and makes the darkness disappear. But the sun *does* rise. Be thankful for that. Then you will be ready to raise the shades.

To be a Christian is to live in the sunrise. Morning comes, but so does night. Still the night is never so dark that it does not vanish before the light of the sun. In a temporal sense there must be changes. The line of faith is not straight, but wavering like the graph on a fever chart. But the course of the sun is not changed by the vicissitudes of earth.

There is a similar relationship between grace and peace. If I know that sunrise is a fact, then I can also know what it means to serve God without fear.

Without fear? Is that possible? Here on earth where we weep and sigh? Where accidents and tragedies abound? Where evil troubles us, and where death awaits? Without fear? Isn't that beyond all reason? Yes, if we were left to ourselves. But Jesus has given us the answer; we are not left to ourselves.

Then let the light in! Because of God's infinite compassion, the light streams in upon us from our Lord Jesus Christ.

The light has come to us on earth;
Do you think that you believe?
Have you thought about the worth
Of God's gifts that you receive?
From Christ's mercy radiance streams;
Has your own soul felt its beams?
Can you find a place apart
For light to dwell within your heart?

BRORSON

24

He Bore Our Guilt

"He was wounded for our transgressions, he was bruised for our iniquities: the chastisement of our peace was upon him, and with his stripes we are healed" (Is. 53:5, KJV). When we read these words from the Old Testament, our thoughts turn naturally to what happened on Golgotha when Jesus Christ was crucified.

"He was *wounded*." The expression reminds us that a battle was being fought on Golgotha. The spiritual powers of good and evil were met in decisive conflict.

"Now is the judgment of this world; now shall the prince of this world be cast out" (John 12:31, KJV). Jesus had spoken these words to his disciples as his time drew near. On the Friday of the crucifixion, the devil gathered all his powers of evil, but in the end, he was disarmed. He could only wound, not win. But wound he did. The disciples had fled; the leaders of the people were in despair. Lies and terror were abroad. And Jesus was alone. He was wounded. But he prayed to his Father, "Forgive them, for they know not what they do!" For our sakes he endured until he had won the victory.

"He was *bruised* for our iniquities." During the three last, dreadful hours of Jesus' life, evil launched a fearful attack, beyond the power of man to realize what was happening. "My God, my God, why hast thou forsaken me?" Jesus cried. The enemy enveloped him in darkness: "You are forgotten now," he taunted; "forgotten by men and forgotten by God. They have all forsaken you, without exception. Even God. You made the wrong choice, and you will sink into oblivion, while I win my victory." Jesus was *bruised.*

But he fought through it. As his head sank, he called to God out of the darkness, "My God!" And then the light broke through, "Father, into thy hands I commend my spirit." It all happened for our sake, and all that we can do is to express our gratitude.

"The chastisement of our peace was upon him." In Luther's exposition of the second article of the Catechism, he says, "He [Christ] has redeemed me, a lost and condemned sinner, purchased and delivered me from all sins and from the power of the devil." He *has* done it. It is finished. For the sake of Jesus, God looks upon us with favor; and when the devil would accuse us, we can point to Christ as our deliverer. The battle is over, and one day the "head of the serpent" will be bruised. (Gen. 3:15.)

It is hard for the human mind to accept and understand the redemption of man through the suffering of Christ. It can be accepted only by faith. "The chastisement of our peace was upon him," and our salvation is secured because we have attained peace with God through our Lord Jesus Christ.

"With his stripes we are healed." What does it mean? It means that our mortal wound has been healed. No one is condemned because of sin; only unbelief can cause Jesus to have died in vain. It means that we know love will conquer in the end. In seeming weakness the great victory was won. Jesus disarmed the powers of evil, and vanquished his antagonist. In that knowledge we can fight our battles with good courage.

"With his stripes we are healed." The love of God sheds light upon suffering. No matter how dark or how baffling life may be, candles are lit for us. We can see Christ's footsteps in the darkness; and when we cannot see the path before us, we can hear his voice calling, "Follow me!" We talk softly about our experiences; but whoever has stood in faith with Christ at Calvary has caught a glimpse of the light that was kindled there. We are healed by his stripes.

We cannot solve the riddle of the cross. But we can thank our crucified and risen Savior for bearing our guilt.

O Jesus Christ, God's Son and Lamb
Who cleared our way to heaven,
You took our guilt and bore our shame,
That our souls might be forgiven.
For us you died, for us you rose;
In faith your blood forever flows,
A precious, blessed fountain.

GRAESK SALME

25

When the Enemy Tempts

"Lead us not into temptation." There is something puzzling about this petition from the Lord's Prayer. God does not tempt anyone to do wrong. We cannot say that we are tempted by God; why then should we pray, "Lead us not into temptation"?

The petition does remind us that there are two powers striving for mastery over us. We have not solved the mystery of evil. What is its origin? No one has given a satisfactory answer; but the philosopher Pascal says that even though the doctrine of the fall of man and of inherited sin presents many problems, our existence would be even more puzzling without this teaching. But this seems clear—evil is a hostile power that attacks us from without.

It is worth noting, moreover, that the word we translate as "temptation" also is used to denote "put to the test." The two forces competing for mastery over the human soul labor—one for us, the other against us. One power works to help us win the victory, the other works for our defeat. God tests us in order to cleanse, purify, and sanctify us; and he is with us in our hour of trial. But Satan digs pits for us to fall into and then deserts us when darkness closes around us.

We should remember also that Jesus, who taught us the words, "Lead us not into temptation," has himself been tempted. In Luke's account of Jesus' temptation in the wilderness, we read that "when the devil had ended all the temptation, he departed from him for a season" (Luke 4:13, KJV). He returned later on with his fiercest temptation. Because Jesus himself was tempted and had suffered, he can come to our aid when we are tempted.

But even after these explanations, the wording of this sixth petition of the Lord's Prayer still presents problems. One further hint may be of some help.

Isn't there a close relationship between the sixth and seventh petitions? It may help to consider them together. "Lead us not into temptation, but deliver us from evil!" Take us by the hand. *Lead* us! Be near to help when the enemy tempts! Do not let him win the victory! Help us to stand in the day of evil and the hour of temptation! Keep us from falling away when evil desires flare up! Keep the spark of faith alive when defeat seems close at hand! *Lead* us!

The enemy's purpose in temptation is to "derail" us, to get us off the right track. He tosses smoke bombs to bewilder us. He fixes our gaze on the present. Perhaps we discover before us something glittering and bright. "Take it!" says our tempter. "Try it just this once."

Perhaps some great difficulty looms before us. We

have suffered a loss, something we can never recover. Or a sorrow that makes us ask, "Why? Why?" Bitterness may slip in, gradually infecting mind and soul. Satan has slid an obstruction between us and God. We can no longer see our Lord.

Or the enemy may exploit our disappointments in the struggle with prayer and faith. "If you believe in God," he says, "you have a right to expect help. You haven't received help. Your faith is only in your imagination. You are struggling to overcome evil, but you aren't winning. Why not? If there is a God, and if he is interested in saving you, why doesn't he intervene to rescue you? Just take it easy!"

You can see how crafty our enemy is. He knows where we are weakest, when we are tired and discouraged. Sometimes he lies in wait at our place of prayer, or at the communion table. Often he comes at night in the hours of darkness. He makes use of every opportune moment. He is always trying to rob us of the joy of our faith. So be on guard!

Evil can be defeated only by our use of God's Word. "Take . . . the sword of the Spirit, which is the Word of God" (Eph. 6:17). But remember that the enemy can also quote Scripture. He is well versed in it. Never try to negotiate with him, but make your confession of faith: "I renounce the devil and all his works and all his ways." He is a liar, and he must be resisted. Take your stand on the Word of God. And pray sincerely, "*Lead us,* lead us not into temptation, but deliver us from evil!"

Hold fast to your baptismal vow,
And let the old Fiend sputter;
The powers of Hell may tremble now
At truths God's Word can utter.
Just pray the prayer our Lord has taught,
And Satan's power shall come to naught
As you do battle bravely.

MIKKEL JENSEN

26

Bound or Free

Freedom is the best word in the world. The statement is true if we understand it correctly. Actually, none of us are free. We are all bound. We can see it in every aspect of life, from the smallest matters to those of great importance.

For instance, we are anxious not to seem different from the people around us. We want to seem up to date and to follow the crowd. Follow the fashion, or move out! Why? Is the opinion of others so really important?

We play the fool for one another and do not dare to give expression to our true feelings. Bound—so that others can know what we do and play around with. But after all, how much do we really know about one another? Some who seem aggressive and daring are afraid to open the doors of their homes lest others should see what they are hiding. Some withdraw into their shells, and loneliness haunts them.

Self-analysis does not help us. We want to be good. Then why aren't we? Again we hear Paul speaking: "For the good that I would, I do not; but the evil which I would not, that I do" (Rom. 7:19, KJV). Why? Because we are bound.

Have you ever watched a sparrow flying around in a room? Skilled flier that it is, it cannot find its way out. It turns to the ceiling, the walls, and the doors, up and down, back and forth; but it cannot get out. Such is our own situation; our flutterings are futile.

There is a better way of living. We believe in God and we know his promises; there is no other place for us to go but to Jesus Christ. Why aren't we filled daily with abounding joy? Why do we try to hide our Christian faith? Why can't we show plainly that we are children of light?

If we are to become free men and women, we must realize that the way out of bondage is found in quietness before God. There is only one who can speak the word of redemption for us who are in bondage—Jesus.

It is strange and tragic that so many of us know his work of redemption, but find that it means so little to us. Unless we accept it, it cannot redeem us. He says, "Fear not!" but we are choked with fears. He says, "My peace I give unto you." But we feel no peace. We are shut in, and his word does not reach us.

To repeat, then, the way to redemption is found in that stillness in which we can open our hearts and minds to Christ and listen to his words of salvation. Our redemption is linked inseparably with the only one who can free us from our bonds.

The conditions of freedom are ready, but to an appalling degree we involve ourselves with the mortal lie that if we take liberties for ourselves, we are free. No, that is the way one remains a slave. Freedom cannot be seized. No man can have it unless it is given to him from heaven.

Redemption has its root in the forgiveness of sins. Paul states it plainly when he talks about what God has given us through Jesus Christ. "In him we have redemption, through his blood, the forgiveness of our trespasses, according to the riches of his grace" (Eph. 1:7).

Brorson expresses the same thought in one of his hymns. "Verily, he took my part; therefore you are *free,* my heart." Set free! Redeemed! Not under judgment, but free!

The more fully we accept this message of redemption, the more surely it will find expression in true liberty, and the more closely we shall be bound to Christ.

The story is told of a rich merchant who traveled in the Orient. He came to a place where a slave-trader stood with a band of young women who were to be sent away in bondage. One unhappy young woman was looking in all directions as if searching for help. The merchant, obeying an impulse, paid a large sum of money to set her free. When the slave-trader told the girl she was free, she cast herself at the merchant's feet and said, "If it is true that you have paid for me and that I may go where I please, then you must know that my prayer is that I may serve you all my life."

So it is with real freedom. It wants to live in the service of the Redeemer.

To thee, Lord, I will give
My soul, my life, my all;
My Master, while I live,
Who bought me when a thrall.
Lord Jesus, dwell in me!
With lips and heart I'll sing
Hosannas to my King
In whose service I am free!

KINGO

27

Teach Us to Pray

Is it perhaps true that the saying of evening prayer is the last cord to be cut in the relationship between God and man? Other ties probably go first. Perhaps they never existed. Holy Communion, for instance. One took Communion on the Sunday following confirmation and therewith—for many—this chapter was finished. Church attendance? Yes, perhaps one attends now and then, mostly at Christmas or Easter. Bible reading is neglected. But the custom of evening prayer is not dropped easily. One repeats the Lord's Prayer.

What is the reason? Why does the thread of prayer outlast the other ties? Is fear the main reason? Is it because we suspect that "there are more things between heaven and earth than are dreamed of" in our philosophizing? Is there a hidden need for reliance on someone or something greater than one's self? Or is prayer just a habit that has not yet been broken? It is hard to say what the reason is; but since evening prayer is often man's last expression of relationship with God, prayer must be of fundamental importance.

Prayer is a normal function of life. We are created not just to be working, reasoning beings; we are created to pray. Man's distinguishing characteristic is not just that he can walk upright, but that he can also bend his knees to worship his Creator. Man's supreme advantage over other creatures finds expression in the fact that he can acknowledge his weakness and confess it to God in prayer. If we do not pray, we are not living normal lives.

Prayer means, first of all, coming to God with one's weakness. The troubles of life bring us to our knees. We must go somewhere with our problems. To whom shall we go? Even the strong and the wise cannot help us. They do not understand us. "When you pray, go into your room and shut the door and pray to your Father" (Matt. 6:6). Your Father understands you; he cares for you; and he can help you. We are not beggars asking for alms. We are children who come to their Father, confident that he knows what his children need.

Prayer means giving thanks for the good things we have received. If we are to pray aright, the giving of thanks must be an important part of our prayers. But our prayers are often marked more by our asking for help than by giving thanks. Perhaps this is one reason why we so often ask if prayer avails. It can avail. Jesus said so, plainly. "Everyone that asks receives." But we must remember that prayer and thanksgiving belong together.

Prayer also means confessing our guilt. In the Lord's Prayer the fourth and fifth petitions are joined by "and." "Give us this day our daily bread, and forgive us our debts as we forgive our debtors." Jesus is reminding us that forgiveness is the principal need in our lives. We must have bread daily if we are to live; and we need forgiveness if we are to live with assurance. When we fold our hands in prayer, it is good to remember that God does not owe us anything. We are the debtors. Nowhere is it written that if we just realize that we are not very good, we'll get to heaven in the end. But it is written, "If we *confess* our sins, he is faithful and just to forgive our sins, and to cleanse us from all unrighteousness" (1 John 1:9, KJV).

Prayer means communing with God. "Unto thee, O Lord, do I lift up my soul. O my God, I trust in thee" (Ps. 25:1, 2a, KJV). The words appear more than once in the Old Testament. We come to God not only to ask for his gifts, but to talk things over with him. "Just knock," said Jesus, expressing the essence of prayer. Prayer brings us into fellowship with God.

Prayer means being with God in silence. Some complain that it is not easy to wait before God in silence. It is not easy, but necessary. "Truly my soul waiteth upon God: from him cometh my salvation" (Ps. 62:1, KJV).

Be still before the Lord, my soul,
Before the Lord who comforts me.
Pleasures of the world console
Briefly, then away they flee.
Forget, my soul, griefs here below;
Soon peace of God in heaven we'll know.

BRORSON

28

Effectual Prayer

A wise man has said that through prayer we delve out the treasures that the Gospel of Jesus has allowed us to see with the eyes of faith. Just as the earth has riches which cannot be brought out except by thought and effort, there are also spiritual riches which cannot be ours unless we pray. There is no use in questioning the necessity for prayer. All objections have been overruled by the two words, "Jesus prayed."

"Does it do any good for us to pray?" some may ask. "We have tried to pray, but nothing happened. Is it any wonder that a man gets tired of praying and gives up when nothing happens? Why doesn't God hear my prayer? I know my prayers are poor and fumbling, but I try to be honest in them. What is wrong when they are not answered?"

No honest prayer is spoken in vain. A fundamental law of prayer is presented in the seventh chapter of Matthew. Jesus is speaking. "Ask, and it will be given you; seek and you will find; knock, and it will be opened to you. For everyone who asks receives, and he who seeks finds, and to him who knocks, it will be opened" (Matt. 7:7, 8). The words cannot be misunderstood. No honest prayer is offered in vain.

But it is evident that prayer must be more than an experiment or something to be used only in an hour of distress. Prayer and faith belong together. "Without faith it is impossible to please him. For whoever would draw near to God must believe that he exists and that he is the reward of those who seek him" (Heb. 11:6). Without faith, prayer is only an experiment. Conversely, faith without prayer is only an impersonal acceptance of opinions. Prayer and faith cannot be separated.

"So my weak faith is the reason my prayers aren't answered!" you say. "But what am I to do about it? One cannot compel faith. I am praying because I need help in order to believe."

First of all, let us make it clear that prayer is not a performance by which we try to force God to help us. "Your Father knows what things you need before you ask him," Jesus said (Matt. 6:7b). God is not unwilling to give. He is generous, open-handed. And prayer is not something by which we seek the favor of God, but an attitude of open hands with which we receive what God is longing to give us. It is worth noting that some of those who came to Jesus in prayer spoke only a single sentence. Not a long and perfectly formed prayer, not a strong declaration of confidence; not an explanation, but a single sincere sigh from the heart: "Have mercy on us, O Lord, thou Son of David!" (Matt. 20:30, 31). "Lord, help me!" (Matt. 15:25). "Lord, remember me when thou comest into thy kingdom!" (Luke 23:42. All KJV.)

Then we must expect that our enemy will put many hindrances in the way when we begin to pray. He tries to stop us quickly. "What good does it do?" he whispers. "Perhaps God has grown tired of you. Or perhaps your prayers are nothing but empty words. What do you really expect to accomplish with your prayers? Do you think you can influence God? Isn't God love? And isn't he unchangeable? Doesn't he already know all about you?" So Satan creeps up on us, trying to discourage us. But he is a liar; he must be repulsed. Jesus has said that it helps to pray, and we must believe him.

Prayer and perseverance belong together. Keep on praying! Knock again! God is not unwilling. When he is silent or tarries long before he answers our prayer, it is for some good reason. While we are waiting, the cord binding us to him is being held more securely. We should remember that God has not promised to give us everything that we desire, but the promises he has made, he will keep. Something happens when we pray. Through our prayers we become partakers of God's blessing.

None need suffer shame if only
They will put their trust in God.
Sorry, sickly, frightened, lonely?
Pray and trust and onward plod.
Just remember that he sees you,
Oh, he knows when troubles tease you;
If your woes to him you tell,
He will keep you, guard you well!

BRORSON

29

Our Pattern for Prayer

Is the Lord's Prayer enough? Do we need to pray more than this one prayer which we learned in childhood? If we cannot formulate a prayer in our own words, isn't it all right to consider everything included in the Lord's Prayer?

Well, there is some justification for doing so. The Lord's Prayer does cover our needs. But some feel that they want to speak more fully with God about their particular needs. Who would want to leave his own children out of his prayers? Or friends in trouble or illness? Is it not natural also, to want to talk to God about the joys or sorrows of the moment? Jesus, too, mentioned some special petitions for us to include in our prayers; such as, "Pray therefore the Lord of the harvest to send out laborers into his harvest" (Matt. 9:38; Luke 10:2b).

But the Lord's Prayer is the pattern for all our prayers, and it is well if our prayers are in agreement with it. This is not always easy. We should be especially careful not to let the Lord's Prayer become something that we repeat without thinking about its meaning. It is a good rule not to say the prayer too fast.

"Our Father, who art in heaven . . ." These opening words recognize the fact that our relationship with

God is like that of father and children. Since God is our Father, we may talk with him. And since he is our Father, he has the right to our confidence.

Luther's explanation of the opening words of the Lord's Prayer is good: "God hereby tenderly encourages us to believe that he is truly our Father and that we are truly his children so that we may boldly and confidently come to him in prayer as beloved children come to their dear father." God invites us to believe just that.

In the Lord's Prayer the order of the different petitions is not accidental. The prayer should always be given in the right order from beginning to end.

The first three petitions deal respectively with God's name, God's kingdom, and God's will. Only after voicing these three petitions do we come to the ones that are concerned with our daily lives. "But seek first his kingdom and his righteousness, and all these things shall be yours as well" (Matt. 6:33). These words of Jesus confirm all the petitions in the Lord's Prayer. The order should not be changed.

The conditions of life keep changing. There are good times and hard times. Situations arise when we need to be especially concerned with the fifth petition: "And forgive us our debts, as we also have forgiven our debtors" (Matt. 6:12). There are days when we must struggle with the third petition: "Thy will be done." And there are moments when the last two petitions are the most urgent: "Lead us not into temptation, But deliver us from evil." It is helpful to pause after each petition and think about its content. The prayer contains so much of great significance that we should never cease to meditate upon it.

Should we say the Lord's Prayer every day? There are no set rules. But each day as we pray we should follow the path which the Lord's Prayer points out. This prayer is the pattern for all prayer. It teaches us that we need not use many words, but that we should be definite in our requests to God.

An elderly woman who was hard of hearing was present at an open-air service, taking a seat in the front row so that she could hear the speakers. She listened carefully to the pastor's opening prayer. She evidently thought his prayer was too full of empty words. Finally she interrupted, saying, "Pray to God for something definite, man!" We can make specific requests if we have the right conception of the Lord's Prayer. Pray for something. Pray directly. Pray like children talking to a loving father.

With the Lord's Prayer, as with all true prayer, we must try to be co-workers with God in the fulfillment of our petitions. Pray and work! Pray as if everything depended on God! Work as if everything depended on you! Both are important. There is no sense in praying, "Thy kingdom come!" if we do not lift a finger to help his kingdom come. It is illogical to pray, "Lead us not into temptation," if we do not try to be on guard ourselves. We must be co-workers with God in our prayers.

We find in the letter to the Hebrews some words that inspire us to pray, at the same time that they remind us that we are "ashes and dust"; "Let us then with confidence draw near to the throne of grace, that we may receive mercy and find grace to help in time of need" (Heb. 4:16).

When we pray, we are standing before the throne of grace. This we must remember. We come like God's beloved children, not doubting that there is power in the folded hands.

When an honest soul in Jesus' name
Would fold his hands in prayer,
The words may die on his lips in shame
That "dust to dust" is our share.
When pity strikes an aching chord,
This heartache you can banish;
Just whisper soft the Prayer of our Lord
And grief, in rejoicing, will vanish.

GRUNDTVIG

30

Thy Will Be Done

Over the road that Jesus had to travel were inscribed two words, "I must." In everything that he said or did he was constrained by this compelling motive, *I must*. "How is it that you sought me? Did you not know that I *must* be in my Father's house?" These were the words of the twelve-year-old Jesus when Mary and Joseph found him at last in the Temple (Luke 2:49). "Let it be so," said Jesus to John the Baptist at the River Jordan, "for thus it is fitting for us to fulfil all righteousness" (Matt. 3:15).* And at one time when the crowds would have detained him, Jesus replied, "I *must* preach the good news of the kingdom of God to other cities also; for I was sent for this purpose" (Luke 4:43). To Zacchaeus up in the fig tree outside Jericho, Jesus said, "I *must* stay at your house today" (Luke 19:5). "*Ought* not Christ to have suffered these things, and to enter into his glory?" (Luke 24:26, KJV), he asked the two disciples on the way to Emmaus on Easter afternoon. These are just a few of the citations that indicate how the words *I must* seemed to be a guiding light in the path of Jesus' life.

When we pray the third petition of the Lord's

*A literal translation of the corresponding verse in a Danish version reads, "This we *must* do to fulfil all that is for righteousness."

Prayer, "Thy will be done," we are being reminded that God has a plan for human life and that the whole plan is in accordance with his will.

There are situations in which it is impossible for us to see just what the will of God is. We wonder, "What is the meaning of this? What shall I do now? Why am I led along this road?" We do not know. But that does not alter the fact that God has a purpose for our whole life. It is only as we take the long view of life that we can pray meaningfully, "Thy will be done."

We know what God wants. He is thinking always of our salvation, and his acts are determined by the love that was revealed in Jesus Christ. Much that happens in our lives is *not* according to the will of God. So we must be careful about saying, "Well, it had to be!" Perhaps it didn't. But even in these situations God can come to help us in accordance with his will. Remember this when you pray. "Thy will be done." These words are not a prayer of resignation, to be said with bowed head, expecting the worst. It is a brave prayer of faith in which we yield ourselves to him who always wants the best for us and who is almighty in power.

J. P. Mynster's book, *Meditations on Christian Doctrines,* has a chapter entitled "The Obligation to Believe." Mynster writes, "Early and late, in peace and in war, I will remind myself of my obligation to believe in God and in him whom God has sent . . . I want to believe. If others believe with me, I will rejoice in their fellowship. If they do not believe, I will believe alone; and I will not be ashamed if fools mock me." Such is the situation of any man who is convinced in his heart of the compelling power of the two words, *I must.*

With this conviction comes also an understanding of the relationship between obedience and cheerfulness, or fearlessness. Two passages in the gospel of John express this relationship. When men were concerned that Jesus might be hungry, he replied, "My food is to do the will of him who sent me, and to accomplish his work" (John 4:34). Later Jesus says, "He who sent me is with me; he has not left me alone, for I always do what is pleasing to him" (John 8:29). Because he walked the way of obedience, bound by his "I must," he was never alone. Even in Gethsemane an angel came from heaven to strengthen him.

We are inclined to think of prayer as a means of getting something from God. We do get something. "Prayer brings God's peace from heaven to earth." But we must not forget that true prayer consists in giving ourselves to God. We seek God to be with God, not to obtain his gifts. Even less do we pray to have our wills prevail. "Thy will be done," we say. That is what we *must* say.

Let me earnestly endeavor
Thy good pleasure to fulfill;
In me, thro' me, with me ever,
Lord, accomplish thou thy will.
Call me not until I'm built
In thy likeness, as thou wilt.

ELIZABETH LUDAMILIA

31

A New Life

"If any one is in Christ, he is a new creature; the old has passed away, behold, the new has come" (2 Cor. 5:17). "We were buried with him by baptism into death, so that as Christ was raised from the dead by the glory of the Father, we too might walk in newness of life" (Rom. 6:4).

Some will shake their heads at these words, saying that they do not understand them, "for that is theology!" What does it mean to become a new creature? What does it mean to walk in newness of life?

Do you remember the story of Nicodemus who came to Jesus by night? Perhaps reviewing his experience (John 3:1-21) will help us find answers to the questions above.

Why did he come? He was a religious man, and he held God in reverence. He was a seeker after truth, one who pondered over life. But he was evidently on his guard against Jesus. Why had he come? Did he himself know why? Nicodemus began in a patronizing fashion. That was not wise. When Jesus spoke of the necessity of being born again, Nicodemus asked a naive question, "How can a man be born again when he is old?"

Then Jesus took charge of the conversation. He knew he was speaking to a man without roots, without peace, and without courage. He treated him firmly, and the old Nicodemus disappeared. His mind was filled with new ideas, for Jesus was speaking of a new life which Nicodemus wanted to have.

When we speak about a man's becoming a new creature, it is obvious that he must make a fresh start. This new beginning can come only from God.

It is common for extremists in religion to want to build a tower of Babel from earth to heaven. It cannot be done. Jesus did not come to deliver plans for the erection of a new Babel. He came to clear the ground of old errors and so to make possible a fresh start for man.

So he said, in effect, to Nicodemus, do you remember the story about the Israelites who had been bitten by servants? And how they were saved? Do you remember the serpent of brass which was put up on a pole? Those who had been bitten by the serpents needed only to lift up their eyes to look at the brass serpent in order to be healed. There was nothing else they needed to do. (See Num. 21:7-9.)

One day, Jesus said to Nicodemus, a cross will be lifted up and salvation will be on that cross. For "as Moses lifted up the serpent in the wilderness, even so must the Son of Man be lifted up, that whosoever believeth in him should not perish, but have eternal life" (John 3:14, 15, KJV).

This is the new beginning, and God made it possible for us.

In the sacrament of Baptism, the matter is explained to each individual in these words: "Accept the symbol of the holy cross as a sign and token that you believe on the crucified Lord Jesus Christ!" We are baptized into a new life on the basis of forgiveness, and we are freed from the power of death and the devil. The old has passed away; behold, all things have become new.

Grundtvig speaks in one of his hymns about the joy of the living. The expression is not explained easily. The joy of the living is our rejoicing in what God has given. We rejoice in working with God's Word; rejoice at being in his presence and walking in his way; rejoice in resisting whatever would destroy our life; rejoice in seeking strength at the Lord's table; rejoice in doing the will of God.

Christianity is not a kind of life insurance policy drawn up in fear. It is a whole new life, in which the inner man is strengthened and death is conquered.

A whole new life—in Christ. Only in him. If we examine ourselves, we find only the old. In ourselves we have nothing. In him, life!

"If any one is in Christ, he is a new creature." He has reason to sing songs of praise.

O Jesus dear! O Savior mild!
Make thou of me thy loving child,
Thy blessed name revering!
Remove what Adam's is and mine.
And open wide to what is thine,
My heart, my eyes, and hearing.

P. C. Kierkegaard

32

When It Is Time to Wait

Periods of waiting come to all of us, usually as the result of sickness or adversity. We have been busy. The tempo of living goes up and up. There is no end to the things we want to do. Suddenly the boom is lowered. Stop! Wait! We are not asked whether we have time to wait. But we may be asked if we know how to wait—how to make good use of this waiting period.

We must realize that there are some hazards connected with a period of inactivity. Let's begin with a simple illustration from everyday life. We are sitting near the radio in the evening waiting for a program to be broadcast—a lecture or a concert that we have been looking forward to. There are only a few minutes left. The announcement comes. We are tuned to the right station. Everything is in order. Then the signal fades. What has happened? Technical difficulties? Nothing happens. It is time for the broadcast, but no sound comes over. A broken connection? Too bad!

One danger of a long waiting period is the risk of broken connections. When life goes against us and hope wavers, some connections in our spiritual life may falter or break. Then panic comes, and fear overwhelms us. We beat the air—in vain. Our world is collapsing about us, and we can't understand it at all.

There are days when God seems far away. Wickedness and distress are so real and close that it is hard to sense any other reality. Where is God? Is there God at all? Is there anything in the world except misery and pain? A connection has been broken.

Perhaps good friends come to call, hoping to cheer us up. They give us advice. "Just wait awhile. Take it easy, now. You'll see, this will all pass over." But for a man whose life has been almost shattered, it is hard even to listen to these attempts at consolation. Is it any wonder that one feels panicky? But one can learn how to wait in patience.

It is important to learn it early. We are likely to think of a time of convalescence as a period of lost time. The days pass. We think we cannot afford to spend them just sitting and waiting. We have forgotten that times of waiting can be times of ripening. God has a purpose in everything.

Brorson is not in sympathy with deep-drawn sighs. "Hard times walk with slow feet," he says to the down-hearted; "you will catch up only by waiting, only by waiting—till summer comes." Yes, that is why it is so important to use the time of waiting in the right way.

In the Old Testament we often meet the expression, "Wait on the Lord!" Waiting on the Lord, or for the Lord, means more than sitting with idle hands in the waiting-room of boredom. He who really waits on the Lord knows that there can be spiritual activity and excitement in just waiting. "I will look to the Lord," says the prophet Micah; "I will wait for the God of my salvation; my God will hear me. . . . When I sit in darkness, the Lord will be a light to me" (Mic. 7:7, 8b). Micah had learned something about the right use of the time of waiting.

If we do not let our communication lines with God be broken, we can wait with patience for his calls to us. The time of waiting may become a time of rebirth. While we are waiting, something is being left with us; we begin to see clearly truths that had been hidden; new bonds of understanding are established between us and God; and we begin to understand what it means to say that God works while we wait.

"Wait on the Lord: be of good courage, and he shall strengthen thine heart: wait, I say, on the Lord" (Ps. 27:14, KJV).

Just wait, dear Soul, until the morning,
Wait for him who is ever true!
Even before you meet great sorrow
God with his comfort is waiting for you.
He has promised, wherever a few
Faithful have gathered—even two—
"There in the midst of you I will be,
Waiting to help those who wait for me!"

GRUNDTVIG

33

Confidence

Some people have sunny dispositions and are able to find a way through any difficulty. Others are inclined to see all things through dark glasses. Some rejoice over every good day; others fret in chronic restlessness. Some people are superficial and take any situation as it comes; others are brooding and fearful. Human temperaments differ, and no one can do much to change his natural disposition.

But when the Bible talks about *confidence,* as it often does, it is speaking about something that all of us may possess, no matter what our temperaments are. Whether Paul had a cheerful or melancholy disposition, we do not know. But we do know that from his prison he could write, "I can do all things through Christ, which strengthened me" (Phil. 4:13, KJV).

The confidence of which the Bible speaks is not dependent on the nature of our temperaments nor on whether, so far as circumstances go, we lead a happy life. It comes from something quite different. Let us see what the Bible says about it.

First, though, let us emphasize again the fact that the Bible is the most realistic book in all literature. It describes the world as it really is and reveals man as he is. "In the world you will have tribulation" (John 16:33). ". . . It is appointed for men to die once, and after that comes judgment . . ." (Heb. 9:27). This is lucid language. "You . . . who are evil," says Jesus (Matt. 7:11). He speaks of the prince of this world, who is a liar, and of the perils of life. No one can rightly say that the Bible misleads us about the realities of life.

Fortunately, along with these pictures of the world and mankind, we are given clear directions concerning a confidence that can defy reality.

What does this confidence depend upon? If we want confidence, we must study the Word of God. Even when our own experiences seem contrary to the teachings of the Word, they cannot abrogate the promises God has established with Jesus Christ. As to our own experiences, of course this question is always in order: Was my own attitude right in this instance?

The Bible says that confidence is inseparable from the conviction that God is with us in everything we do. "Be strong and of good courage; be not frightened, neither be dismayed: for the Lord your God is with you wherever you go" (Josh. 1:9). The promise given to Joshua still speaks to us today. Everything rests in the hands of God our Father. Our assurance, then, depends upon our faith in our omnipotent Father.

The Bible says that confidence is based on the assurance that our sins are forgiven. "If God is for us, who is against us? He who did not spare his own Son but gave him up for us all, will he not also give us all things with him?" (Rom. 8:31.) These are strong words. When we are anxious and discouraged, we reach for help that is tangible and near. But God's Word says that through our faith in the forgiveness of sins, it is possible for us to breathe freely. When we actually realize what it means to have peace with God through our Lord Jesus Christ, we are on the way to enjoying true confidence.

In Jesus' name we have *access* to God. This we must believe. " . . . Jesus Christ our Lord, in whom we have boldness and confidence of access through our faith in him," Paul wrote (Eph. 3:11c, 12) when he was in prison. Through Christ we, though undeserving, have access to God's grace. Only one who has been pardoned can be confident. Such is the teaching of the Bible about Christian confidence.

When the adversities of life wear down our assurance and we are utterly despondent, we can turn to God. His door is open and his promises are sure.

Thou best dost know my need,
O Lord, so tender;
My happiness, my life, indeed,
I now surrender.
And what will serve me best from day to day
Thou canst foresee;
That give to me.
Dear God, direct my way!

KINGO

34

On Paths of Loneliness

In Martin A. Hansen's book, *The Liar*, a school teacher who is the main character comments about himself as he nears the end of his life. He says that although he is a man hounded by doubt and unbelief, he nevertheless recognizes a divine force. "But I am too old to make promises that I am not sure I can keep. My flight is over, and the dream has faded. Yes, I can choose my destiny, and I can still flail out, but I cannot grow. I cannot change myself. Only the Creator ['the Button-moulder' is the name he uses] can change a person. My weakness and my sin is great, for I feel the presence of God only when he hits me hard."

There is some worldly wisdom in the words of the school teacher, and many who dare to be honest will agree with him.

We cannot defy the laws of life. They cannot be changed, no matter how many protest against them. "Whatever a man sows, that he will also reap" (Gal. 6:7). We do not like to hear these words, but we cannot change the truth in them.

What causes all the confusion and perplexities in the world today? What causes the anxieties and the great need?

There was a time when everything was "very good." But that was long, long ago.

What happened to change it?

There was a catastrophe. Man rebelled against God and tried to take life into his own hands. We all have had some part in it—the good and the bad, the great and the lowly, the pious and the profane—we are all guilty. "For what I would, that I do not; but what I hate, that I do." I do not understand myself. "I cannot make myself over; everyone knows that."

Two forces are at war in the world, and two wills struggle for mastery in our own minds. We live in a lost Paradise, and there are many wastelands or wildernesses. Some act as if the situation were not serious. "Pshaw," they say, "nothing will happen in our time."

Perhaps disaster will not come in our time. But those who dare to face the truth know that it is not easy to be a member of the human race, and that our days will come to an end sometime. There is no use in being offended or irritated when sin is being discussed. Sin is not errors and shortcomings. It is not grave misdemeanors that bring prison terms. Sin is putting oneself on par with God. Sin is turning one's back on Jesus Christ. Sin is selfishness and disbelief. Because of sin we walk the lonely ways of life.

Where is salvation? The school teacher spoke about the Button-moulder. Let us say, speaking literally, that salvation comes through Jesus Christ, who taught us to pray, "Deliver us from evil."

The good news is that Jesus can come to us in the wastelands. Earth is a lost Paradise, and no one escapes the venomous bite of the serpent. But the cherubim with flaming swords who guarded the gates to the Garden of Eden, will give way before the crucified and risen Christ.

Christ opens the way to Paradise, and he comes to us in the lonely places. He is the One who comes, and we are the ones who go. "I will come to you" (John 14:18), he said on that last evening when his disciples felt certain that he was going away. No, he does not go away. He comes, and he stays.

There are footprints on the lonely way. Jesus has been in the wilderness himself. He has been tempted in all ways, just as we are; but he was without sin. He can say with authority, "Fear not!"

The tempter may meet you on a lonely path. He has great power there. "Give up!" he says. That is how he surprised Elijah in the days of old. The prophet, tired and discouraged, was sitting under a juniper tree in the desert. But God called him back to his task. The worst thing that can happen to us in the wilderness is to fail to guard ourselves against the evil forces that haunt the lonely ways.

"I can choose my destiny," said the schoolmaster. Yes, that we can. We can call upon One who will come to meet us, and we can commit ourselves to him. We can ask him to care for us. To those who follow him, he says, "I give unto them eternal life; and they shall never perish, neither shall any man pluck them out of my hand" (John 10:28, KJV).

Let me feel your helping hand
When my life grows lonely;
And dear Father, near me stand
For I trust you only.
When night and darkness in my breast
With their fears confound me,
Bring your comfort and your rest;
Let your light surround me!

Jakob Knudsen

35

The Last Watch

How shall we be able to face death? The question is one which every human being should be intensely concerned with. Usually people are not. There is usually a great deal of loose talk about death. And many people deliberately put the subject aside because thinking seriously about it might upset their way of living.

Some believe that death is the natural closing of life. Flowers wither and men die. Medical science has learned how to make death practically painless. There is no reason for panic. We'll just sleep away as quietly as the autumn sun fades. That is all there is to it.

Then there are those who dream about some beautiful unknown shore to which we shall all drift some day. No matter whether we have used or misused our lives, the end will be good. And so the casket must be covered with flowers and the candles must be lit so that the cruelty of death can be kept at a distance.

But is this right? Does it help us meet death? No, not in the least.

No one really knows what death is since no one who has experienced it can come back to tell us. But if we face the truth, we realize that the worst thing to do is to try to keep death at a distance by fostering romantic fantasies about it.

We have no material with which to build a bridge over the chasm between the home of the dying and the land of the living. In death all that has been ours is shattered as if by the breakers of a stormy sea. Why people will not admit this fact is incomprehensible.

But how are we, or can we be, able to face death?

At the feasts of the ancient Egyptians, a silent veiled figure was seated to remind the living that they must die. In certain cloisters a grave was left open ready for the next person to die. We behave differently. We cast ourselves into the stream of life; we cling to life; we do everything in our power to prolong life. There is something about this attitude that is good, for life is a precious gift.

But what does the ability to accept death depend upon? The Norwegian pastor, Gustav Jensen, says of his mother, "She was the person to whom I am most deeply indebted. When we talked together about the deepest things in our faith, she said, 'I cannot get along without the Lord Jesus!' " She had the answer.

In the past there was a special name for the last communion, *viaticum,* which means "the traveler's meal," or "food for the tired traveler." The closer we come to the end of the road, the more we need this food. It is always good to take Communion because the sacrament reminds each individual that his sins have been forgiven through the crucified and risen Lord Jesus Christ.

If we are to be able to face death, we must live daily by the Word of God. Jesus said, "Truly, truly, I say to you, if anyone keeps my word, he will never see death" (John 8:51). Jesus has *life,* and he speaks the words that save us from death. No one else can give us lasting consolation. We too must confess, "I cannot get along without Christ."

It is strange that so many will not accept him. He is the only One who can truly say, "Do not be afraid." He is the only One who can say, "Do not weep!" He is the only One that death could not hold. He comes to us who are on our way to the grave, and says, "Let not your hearts be troubled; you believe in God, believe also in me!" (John 14:1.) We are to live with him. He will help us to give the right farewell to the world.

Some years ago on a visit to the hospital, I met a well known, influential man who has now passed away. At the time he was beside himself with concern. His wife was dying in a nearby room. He had been sitting by her bed, and she was pleading for help in her distress. "Please go to her," he implored. "I cannot bear to see her so distrait. She is talking about a hymn which tells of the last night watch. I don't know which hymn it is. Please find it and read it to her."

I found the hymn, "To bid the world farewell," and read it to her. One line asks that death come in the last watch of the night, clad in the garment of one dearly beloved. It is a prayer to the Lord Jesus. He is the only One who can help us meet death.

It is irresponsible for us to speak lightly of death. Death is the enemy of life. But death has been conquered. A bridge can be built from the home of death to the land of the living. But only One can do it. We cannot do it without the Lord Jesus Christ.

Oh, let me in my final hour
Hear from thy own lips the dower
That spirit and life may own:
How good it is in heaven to dwell,
A place for me, oh tell it well,
Within God's sunlit home!

GRUNDTVIG

36

The Wayfarer's Comfort

To live means to be on the road. We are on a journey, and no one of us knows how far he has gone. We come and we go, and then in the end we all go. Kingo has said in an evening hymn, "I am nearer death today than I've ever been before. Time is ever so slowly opening death's door." Such is our lot.

Years ago people used to speak about "the wayfarer's church." The expression is in accord with the Word of God. We are strangers and pilgrims on earth, seeking a home. Here we have no permanent place, but we are looking for one. We are travelers, and some day we shall come to the end of the road.

But he who is called the Father of mercies and of all comfort has set up depots along the way to provide us with what we need from day to day. No one needs to get lost along the way. No one need lack what he needs. No one need fall prey to the enemy.

Let us think a little about the traveler's well being.

Appreciate the gift of life! Make it a rule to thank God for the bright days. Count the blessings you have received. Remember that boredom is one of the seven deadly sins. Do not belittle God's goodness and patience.

But what if the days are not bright or good? What shall I do then? It is not easy to be thankful for living if I am worn out and weary. The day seems grey, and the path is steep when loneliness and sorrow overwhelm me. Then sighing replaces singing.

The Bible tells us that God is mindful that we are dust. He demands nothing unreasonable of us. But you should realize that even when times are hard and the road difficult, you can still find comfort along the way. God's door is always open, and for that reason alone we always have something to be thankful for. Remember, too, that dangers increase when darkness comes.

And then remember that Jesus lives.

Again we are reminded of some lines from one of Kingo's hymns:

Let it not darken evermore!
I do not fear for any other thing;
When dank, dark airs about me pour,
Let Jesus' light in an encircling ring
The gloom allay—his Spirit still a light
Outshining all earth's torches, clear and bright!

KINGO

Jesus lives. His light is "an encircling ring about us." He who came to the two men on the way to Emmaus and interpreted the Scriptures to them will also come to us. He is the same yesterday, today, and forever.

Then, we should all think of those who have gone before us, fighting the good fight and winning the victory.

"Therefore, since we are surrounded by so great a cloud of witnesses, let us also lay aside every weight, and sin that clings so closely and let us run with perseverance the race that is set before us, looking to Jesus, the pioneer and perfecter of our faith" (Heb. 12:1, 2a). With these words, the writer of the letter to the Hebrews encourages us. It is comforting to the wayfarer to know about those who have gone before. They beckon us onward. Keep trying. Do not give up. Do not get tired!

We should also make use of the sacraments.

When we were baptized, God accepted us and gave his Holy Spirit as a pledge of our inheritance. In the days of the old covenant, God chose Israel to be his special people, and because of his choice he was patient with them, even when they were slow to learn. He always had thought of their salvation, and he never lost sight of the goal.

In the new covenant, Jesus chose certain men and women to be near him. He was patient with them, though they, too, were slow to learn. He loved them to the end.

With us our relation with God begins with infant baptism. By virtue of baptismal grace we are introduced to salvation in Jesus' name. When all about us totters and we can see no escape, we take refuge in this baptismal grace. We also partake of the Lord's supper with a prayer that we may rightly experience the power which is to be found in these gifts.

Finally let the goal of your life cast light upon your way.

When we see the light from our Father's house of many mansions shining brightly, we receive fresh power to persevere. That is the place where we are going; we must not fail to reach it. God grant us a glorious resurrection!

Now opens the Father's house above,
The names of the blest are given:
Lord, gather us there; let none we love
Be missed in the joys of heaven.
Vouchsafe thou us all a place with thee;
We ask through our dear Redeemer.

LANDSTAD